STUDENT COMPANION
A. STEELE BECKER
University of Nebraska at Kearney
JACQUELINE V. BECKER
to accompany

Human Geography
Culture, Society, and Space

Seventh Edition

includes

Study Guide

JOHN WILEY & SONS, INC.

COVER PHOTO: Jochem D. Wijnands/Getty Images

To order books or for customer service call 1-800-CALL-WILEY (225-5945).

To order books or for customer service please, call 1(800)-CALL-WILEY (225-5945).

ISBN 0-471-27204-3

Printed in the United States of America.

10 9 8 7 6 5 4 3 2

Printed and bound Courier Kendallville, Inc.

CONTENTS

HOW TO USE THIS STUDY GUIDE

This study guide has been written to help you in using *Human Geography*, Seventh Edition, in a college-level course to guide you to a better understanding of the important discipline of geography. It is written in a clear and logical manner with the full appreciation of the pressures, scholastic and otherwise, that you will face in an academic environment in the twenty-first century.

Most, if not all, of the material in *Human Geography*, Seventh Edition, will be new to you. This is not a course of simple memorization. Geography is based on the understanding of *concepts* and *relationships*. A college-level text covers more material in greater depth than anything a student is familiar with from high school. Using this guide will help you overcome many of the problems you will encounter in this course.

The Seventh Edition of *Human Geography* has undergone extensive reorganization as well as updating of information to make it a text that is relevant and applicable to the rapidly changing world of the twenty-first century. Issues of gender, political devolution, and environment receive particular attention and have been woven into all parts of the text. Statistical information is the most re-cent that is available and is supported by a wide variety of maps, pictures, and illustrations.

The format for each chapter of the guide is the same. Each chapter begins with a **chapter introduction** that presents expanded discussion on the "Key Points" in the box at the beginning of the chapter. In some cases you will be referred to text material, maps, or illustrations in previous chapters to use in helping you better understand the material currently being covered. This is followed by a **chapter quiz** consisting of **multiple-choice** and **true/false** questions on material from the *entire* chapter, not just the introduction. Answers to the **multiple-choice** and **true/false** questions may be found at the end of the study guide. The last portion of the guide contains a series of **study questions** that are designed to make you think conceptually about the entire chapter.

To gain maximum benefit from the study guide it is important that you read the introduction in the guide *and* the entire chapter *before* it is covered in lecture. The multiple-choice and true/false questions should be used to test your retention of information from these three sources. You should re-read the chapter before attempting the study questions at the end of each chapter in the guide, since these are designed as comprehensive questions to help you tie together facts and concepts. Students are cautioned to remember the guide *is not* a substitute for the text. It *must* be used in combination with the text.

ADDITIONAL HELPFUL HINTS

1. Lectures *must* be attended regularly because your instructor may cover material not in the text. Take good notes and ask questions for clarification.

2. Review lecture notes as soon as possible. Rewrite sections you have trouble reading while the material is still fresh in your mind.

3. Begin reviewing for quizzes and exams well before their scheduled date.

4. Having access to a *current* atlas will be an enormous asset for you in this course.

PART ONE: GEOGRAPHY, CULTURE, AND ENVIRONMENT

CHAPTER 1.   GEOGRAPHY AND HUMAN GEOGRAPHY

CHAPTER INTRODUCTION

Humans are geographers by nature. They can think territorially or spatially and have an awareness of, and curiosity about the distinctive nature of places. Even children possess qualities of geographers, creating carefully mapped realms in tiny places. Places possess an emotional quality, and we all must belong *somewhere*. Humans' insatiable curiosity and the place-centered element within us gave birth to geography as an academic discipline. Conquest and commerce generated a need to know about the world and *pragmatism* was added long ago by traders and explorers. *Geography* literally means "to describe the Earth," and the practical aspects of geography first arose among the Greeks, Romans, Mesopotamians, and Phoenicians.

Divisions
Physical and human geography are two great branches of the discipline, and their origins can be traced to the Greeks and later the Romans. Greek scholars were curious about the world, partic- ularly the physical aspects, and collected information from traders and travelers. The Romans, un- like the Greeks, were empire builders and brought many different cultures under their control. They added to the Greek knowledge of the physical Earth and added information about different cultures they encountered or conquered. By the end of the Roman era, theories about a spherical Earth, latitudinal climatic zones, environmental influences on humans, and humans' role in modifying the Earth were established. The latter two are quite significant because today environmental geography is emerging as a link between human and physical geography.

Traditions
During the twentieth century, geography was marked by four durable traditions: *earth-science* (physical geography); *cultural-environmental* (encompasses a wide range of topics with a difficult, even controversial history); *locational theory* (the spatial focus of the discipline), which has become a modern element of human geography; and *area-analysis* (primarily involving the description of areas and regions), giving rise to what is today called *regional science*. These Four Traditions of Geography were first identified in an article by University of Chicago geographer W.D. Pattison in 1964. He argued that these were the four areas where geographic teaching, research, and other activity were concentrated.

New Themes
In the 1980s, rising concerns about geographic illiteracy in America prompted the National Geo- graphy Society, and several other organizations, to begin campaigns to reintroduce geography into school curricula. In a 1986 publication, the NGS proposed a useful five-theme framework for geography as developed by the Geography Education National Implementation Project (GENIP). Three of the themes correspond to traditions identified earlier: location, human-environment interaction, and regions. As the fourth tradition, the NGS proposed a single word, *place*, because all places on the surface of the Earth have distinguishing human and physical characteristics.

1

A fifth theme, *movement*, refers to the mobility of goods, ideas, and people, an appropriate theme in light of the mobile world we live in today.

Maps

Maps—graphic representations of all or part of the Earth's surface drawn to scale—are the most important tool of geographers. Maps and geography are practically synonymous, and mapmaking (cartography) is as old as geography itself. The spatial perspective is geography's unifying bond and there is no better way to demonstrate insights gained through spatial analysis than through the use of maps. Maps are our "window on the world."

Maps are used to portray the distinctive character of places; their relationship to environmental issues; the movements of people, goods, and ideas; and regions of various types. Maps are used to wage war, make political propaganda, solve medical problems, locate shopping centers, bring relief to refugees, warn of natural hazards—in short, for countless purposes.

Maps are not *always* printed. Everyone has a *mental map*—a map in their mind—that has developed over years of looking at wall maps, atlas maps, and maps in books, magazines, and newspapers. People's perception of places and regions is influenced by their individual mental maps as well as printed maps. Since one's perception of different places is a combination of general information, personal experiences, and what is called "hearsay" in the legal profession, that perception is not always accurate. Look carefully at text Figure 1-9 in your text and you will begin to get some idea of the influence that mental maps and perception of places have on people.

CHAPTER QUIZ

MULTIPLE-CHOICE QUESTIONS

1. This text focuses on human geography. What is the other half of geography called.
   a. environmental
   b. spatial
   c. physical
   d. regional

2. When geographers look at the way places and things are laid out on the cultural landscape, they are taking a:
   a. pattern analysis
   b. distribution measurement
   c. spatial perspective
   d. map measurement

3. Which of the following is **not** true regarding remote sensing:

   a. began with air photography
   b. does not involve satellites
   c. involves aircraft
   d. reveals environmental changes

4. When the National Geographic Society developed what they called the "five themes" of geography they did not specifically include a traditional theme of geography, which is:
    a. location
    b. human-environment
    c. landscape
    d. movement

5. Of the following, which **cannot** be shown on a map.
    a. housing styles
    b. river flow direction
    c. diffusion of disease
    d. relative location

6. What event markedly changed Chicago's relative location (which already had good central-ity).
    a. new interstate highway
    b. more railroads
    c. opening of the St. Lawrence Seaway
    d. new airport

7. Symbols on maps represent many different things. Arrows can show:
    a. direction of migration
    b. numbers of people
    c. intensity of traffic on routes
    d. all of the above

8. The spread of various aspects of culture, such as language, knowledge, skills, religion, etc., from one place to another is called:
    a. distribution
    b. relocation
    c. diffusion
    d. infection

9. Geographers define and delimit a region by:
    a. establishing criteria
    b. walking the region
    c. asking others how they define the region
    d. using climate changes

10. A city is an example of a __?__ region.
    a. formal
    b. functional
    c. perceptual
    d. physical

TRUE/FALSE QUESTIONS

1. Human geography encompasses several subfields and has an environmental component. (TF)

2. Medical geography is not a part of human geography. It belongs to physical geography. (TF)

3. Movement is not an important theme in the study of geography. (TF)

4. The geographical hypothesis of continental drift was actually developed by a climatologist. (TF)

5. The only thing maps can tell us is the absolute location of places. (TF)

6. The relative location of a place can change constantly but only for the better. (TF)

7. A map of worldwide precipitation can show us areas prone to droughts and floods. (TF)

8. The Pacific Ocean affects precipitation on more continental landmasses than any other ocean. (TF)

9. All regions have clear and concise boundaries. (TF)

10. A country is divided into separate regions. No region overlaps another and each is equal in importance. (TF)

STUDY QUESTIONS

1. Why is the spatial perspective so important to geographers? How do patterns and distribution fit into this concept?

2. Make a list of some of the many ways maps are used. Do you understand the importance of relative location as shown in Figure 1-3? Can you find a map of another place that shows good relative location as described in the text?

3. We all live in a region as well as a country or state. What region do you live in? How is it defined? Is it a formal, functional, or perceptual region as defined in your text? Do you have different perceptions about your region?

4. How is your mental map of the city and/or region you live in? After reading the part about mental maps in this chapter, do you think you need to improve yours? Close your eyes. How many Western European nations can you visualize? Go to a map of Europe and see how well you did. Can you accurately visualize the major city locations in your country?

Notes

Notes

CHAPTER 2.   CULTURES, ENVIRONMENTS, AND REGIONS

CHAPTER INTRODUCTION

Culture is an all-encompassing term that defines the tangible lifestyle of a people and their prevailing values and beliefs. The concept of culture is closely identified with anthropology. Over more than a century ago most anthropologists believed that culture was learned. However, recent advances in sociobiology and related fields suggest that certain behaviors may be genetically determined, so that culture has an "instinctive" component as well as a "learned" one. This chapter discusses the development of culture, the human imprint on the landscape, culture and environment, and cultural perceptions and processes. The key points covered in this chapter are outlined below.

Culture and Human Geography
The concept of culture lies at the heart of human geography. Locational decisions, patterns, and landscapes are fundamentally influenced by cultural attitudes and practices. The concept of culture, like the regional concept discussed in the previous chapter, appears to be deceptively simple, but in fact is complex and challenging. The definitions of culture vary widely, as does our use of the word itself, but all refer in one way or another to humans—their development, ideas, and adaptation to the world in which they live.

Components
Culture is made up of four major components. The first of these is a *cultural trait*—a single attribute of a culture—such as eating with certain utensils. The second component is a *cultural complex*—a discrete combination of traits exhibited by a particular culture—such as keeping cattle for different purposes. The third component is a *culture system*—culture complexes with traits in common that can be grouped together—such as ethnicity, language, religion, and other cultural elements. The final component, the *cultural region*—the area within which a particular culture system prevails—is marked by all the attributes of a culture. Cultural regions may be expressed on a map, but many geographers prefer to describe these as *geographic regions* since their definition is based on a combination of cultural properties plus locational and environmental circumstances.

Topics
Key topics in cultural geography include *cultural landscapes*—the human imprint on the Earth's surface. These create a distinct and characteristic landscape that reveals much about the culture presently occupying the area, as well as those that came before. A second key topic focuses on *cultural hearths*—the sources of civilizations from which radiate ideas, innovations, and ideologies. Cultural geographers identify both ancient and modern cultural hearths.

Cultural diffusion—the process by which innovations and ideas spread to other areas—involves several types of diffusion. *Expansion diffusion* may take the form of contagious diffusion, where some item of culture is spread through a local population by contact from person to person. In the case of *hierarchical diffusion*, another form of expansion diffusion, an idea or innovation spreads by trickling down from larger to smaller adoption units. Innovations often leapfrog over wide areas, with geographic distance a less important influence. The early spread of the FAX machine is a good example of this type of diffusion. A third type of expansion diffusion is *stimulus diffusion*, a process where an idea or innovation is not readily adopted by a population but results in local experimentation and eventual changes in the way of doing things. The Industrial Revolution, for example, did not immediately spread to pre- or nonindustrial societies, but did stimulate attempts to mechanize local handicraft production.

The different forms of expansion diffusion take place through populations that are stable. It is the innovation or idea that does the moving. *Relocation diffusion*—the spreading of innovations by a migrating population—involves the actual movement of individuals who have already adopted the idea or innovation, and who carry it to a new, perhaps distant locale, where they disseminate it. The spread of European emigrants around the world during the period of Europeanization is a classic example.

The topic of *cultural perception*—the way that members of a culture view themselves as well as how they view other cultures—is a combination of tangible and intangible elements that help to define the personality of a region. We all have impressions and images of various regions and cultures, even though they may not always be accurate. *Perceptual regions* are intellectual constructs designed to help us understand the nature and distribution of phenomena in human geography. These perceptions are based on our accumulated knowledge about such regions and cultures. Perceptual regions can differ considerably, depending on the individual's mental maps of various communities and cultures.

The final considered topic, *cultural environment*—the relationships between human societies and the natural environment—is complex. Environment affects societies in countless ways from the types of crops grown to the houses they build, but societies also modify their natural environments in ways that range from slight to severe. One thing is certain, however. While human behavior is not controlled by the environment (as the now-defunct concept of environmental determinism suggested), no culture, no matter how sophisticated, can completely escape the forces of nature.

CHAPTER QUIZ

MULTIPLE-CHOICE QUESTIONS

1. When a discrete number of culture traits is combined it is referred to as a culture:
    a. region
    b. complex
    c. realm
    d. system

2. Features placed on the land change its natural look. Geographers call this the cultural:
    a. realm
    b. system
    c. landscape
    d. land change

3. The birth place of a civilization is called a/an:
    a. culture hearth
    b. origin region
    c. agricultural home base
    d. source region

4. When an idea or invention spreads outward from its source area and also remains strong in its source area, it is said to have spread by:
   a. stimulus diffusion
   b. migrant diffusion
   c. expansion diffusion
   d. transculturation

5. When the Spanish overthrew the Aztecs in Mexico, they adopted some of the Aztec ways and ideas. At the same time the Aztecs adopted some of the Spanish ways and ideas. This process is called:
   a. migrant diffusion
   b. relocation diffusion
   c. transculturation
   d. acculturation

6. An assemblage of cultural or geographic regions forms a cultural:
   a. system
   b. realm
   c. complex
   d. trait

7. Perceptual culture regions are:
   a. known to have sharply defined boundaries
   b. different in definition from person to person
   c. defined by using at least three criteria
   d. found only on islands

8. The idea that human cultural behavior is controlled by the environment in which we live is called:
   a. possibilism
   b. environmental ecology
   c. environmental determinism
   d. environmental regional identity

9. The influence of the natural environment on humanity declines:
   a. toward higher latitudes
   b. with increasing technology
   c. in agrarian societies
   d. in urban societies

10. Broad generalizations about the impact of the environment on humans are:
    a. more accurate today than in the past
    b. almost always sustained
    c. rarely sustained
    d. more accurate for traditional agrarian societies

TRUE/FALSE QUESTIONS

1. Culture does **not** include the behavior of people. (TF)

2. The same cultural trait can often be found in more than one culture. (TF)

3. Cultural systems are only found in the developed countries of the world. (TF)

4. Cultural landscapes usually vary from one country to another. (TF)

5. Nomadic people leave a large imprint on their cultural landscape because they keep traveling the same routes over and over. (TF)

6. Culture hearths first appeared in the Eastern Hemisphere. (TF)

7. Most information spread from culture hearths by hierarchical diffusion. (TF)

8. The wheel, after being introduced into Mesopotamia, did not diffuse quickly to Egypt. (TF)

9. Culture regions can become political battlegrounds and even physical battlegrounds because of people's emotional attachments to the land and traditions. (TF)

10. People must learn to live with their physical environment because changing or trying to control it causes problems. (TF)

STUDY QUESTIONS

1. Define the six components of culture. In your own geographical region, can you think of any culture traits that seem to stand out from the normal traits with which you are familiar?

2. After reading about cultural landscapes, can you see signs of how your culture region's landscape has changed over time? If you are attending a college or university away from home, look for material changes in the landscape. Talk to a long-time resident who can tell you about changes that have taken place.

3. Why do you think it is important to study cultural hearths? When you look at Figure 2-4 in your text, can you understand how expansion and relocation diffusion worked in carrying ideas and inventions to distant lands?

4. If you live in a large city, can you see signs of acculturation in ethnic neighborhoods? If you come from a rural environment, is everyone alike or are there ethnic differences that might be evident in the way people layout farm buildings or in house-building styles dating from an earlier time?

5. Look at Figure 2-8 in your text. In which perceptual region is your home state? Does this map fit with your perception of what region you live in? If not, how do you perceive where you live? On what do you base your reasoning?

Notes

Notes

CHAPTER 3.   THE EARTH AS HUMANITY'S HOME

CHAPTER INTRODUCTION

This chapter introduces you to the physical and environmental aspects of the Earth, both past and present, and the impact of human occupancy. It also focuses on the development of humanity during one of the most fascinating geologic epochs, the Holocene. During this epoch, humanity developed socially, politically, and economically. In addition, the number of humans occupying Earth soared. There is much to learn from this chapter, both to lay the foundation for the remainder of the text and to broaden your knowledge of human and Earth history that led to the world we live in today.

Environment

Despite what you may think, the Earth's environment is not stable and environmental change is humankind's constant companion. To understand the geography of culture, it is necessary to understand the complexity of the environment within which humanity lives. Many changes in the environment have occurred since early hunter-gatherers began to exploit the Earth's resources and deal with their environment. The survival of humanity may well depend on an understanding and appreciation of environmental conditions.

Earth's environment frequently changes, and warming and cooling of the planet are natural. Far more of the Earth's surface is water than land, as a glance at any world map will reveal, and only a small percentage of the total surface is suitable for human occupancy. Humanity is quite old, but compared to the age of the Earth, we are recent occupiers. The Earth is currently in the grip of a long series of glacial advances (cooling periods) and retreats (warming periods); modern human civilization emerged during a warm spell between glaciations.

Technological progress notwithstanding, terrain and climate continue to influence the distribution and nature of human life and activity. Compare, for example, text Figure 3-4 (Global Terrain), text Figure 3-5 (World Climates), and text Figure 4-1 (World Population Distribution). Ask yourself why people are where they are **and** why they are **not** in other places. In essence, humans are "where they have always been," relative to terrain and climate. What has changed are the numbers.

Human Development and Innovation

The various stages in Earth history have been divided into periods of geologic time. The most recent geologic time period, the Holocene epoch, refers to the most recent 12,000 plus years of Earth's history. Because of the unique cultural-geographical characteristics of this period of great environmental variation, it is sometimes referred to as "Holocene humanity." Within this short time humanity did what it had not done in previous interglaciations.

Perhaps the single most significant event of the early Holocene was the domestication by humans of plants and animals, which may have occurred nearly simultaneously in areas as far removed as the Middle East and Southeast Asia. Agriculture developed and surpluses were stored for future use. Villages grew larger, towns and cities emerged, and political organization became increasingly complex; inventions multiplied, and tools became more efficient. Certain communities thrived, sometimes at the expense of others. The earliest states appear to have emerged about 5500 years ago in the middle East and southeastern Turkey. The spiral leading toward empires, colonial realms, and global power struggles had begun.

Human Population

Humans have always used *resources* (sometimes defined as anything that humans value), but that use is dependent on, among other things, the number of humans and the technology available to them. The human population growth spiral began during the Holocene epoch. Numbers at the beginning of this epoch have been estimated at between 4 and 8 million. Population growth during the Holocene began slowly at first, then accelerated. Modern humanity is indeed the product of the Holocene epoch.

During the Holocene the Earth changed as never before, not because of geologic forces but because of humanity's humanity. That imprint has become stronger over time, especially over the last 200 years when human population growth and pressure on resources have reached unprecedented levels. This began with the Industrial Revolution in Europe and spread globally during the period of Europeanization and colonialization. During the twentieth century, the Earth especially felt the strains created by the human population. Raw materials were used up at an ever faster rate while the air, water, and land became polluted or damaged. Together, these events have rendered environmental change one of the key issues of the twenty-first century.

CHAPTER QUIZ

MULTIPLE-CHOICE QUESTIONS

1. When America's first lunar astronauts first looked at the Earth, the dominant color they saw was:
   a. blue
   b. green
   c. brown
   d. gray

2. Approximately 70 percent of the land surface of the earth is:
   a. plateaus
   b. desert
   c. tropical forest
   d. ice caps

3. A glacial period was in progress as recently as __?__ years ago.
   a. 6,000
   b. 8,000
   c. 10,000
   d. 20,000

4. Human population growth began during which of the following geologic epochs.
   a. Miocene
   b. Holocene
   c. Paleocene
   d. Pleistocene

5. Cultural geographer Carl Sauer suggested that plant domestication may have begun more than 14,000 years ago in:
   a. Mesopotamia
   b. Mesoamerica
   c. Southeastern Asia
   d. eastern China

6. The development of sedentary and irrigated agriculture and the rise of villages and towns initially occurred in:
   a. Southwest Asia
   b. East Africa
   c. South America
   d. Southeast Asia

7. Ancient Babylon was located on the Euphrates River in present-day:
   a. Iran
   b. Turkey
   c. Iraq
   d. Greece

8. Which of the following human activities transforms more of the Earth's surface than any other.
   a. manufacturing
   b. urbanization
   c. farming
   d. transportation

9. Africa's most populous country is:
   a. Nigeria
   b. Kenya
   c. Egypt
   d. Tanzania

10. The continent which consists mainly of plateaus, and therefore supports fewer people than the single country of India, is:
    a. Australia
    b. Africa
    c. South America
    d. Asia

TRUE/FALSE QUESTIONS

1. Climatic fluctuations during ice ages have little effect on Earth's livable space. (TF)

2. Today Earth is going through the end of an ice age caused by global warming. (TF)

3. The Holocene epoch has been humankind's time of the greatest cultural development. (TF)

4. The Paleolithic period is the latest stage of the Stone Age. (TF)

5. The world's oldest continuous civilization may have started in China. (TF)

6. Domestication of plants and animals kept people nomadic because animals ate all the nearby grass and land was worn out from farming. (TF)

7. The first cities arose in the Fertile Crescent. (TF)

8. Caring for plants is the same as plant domestication. (TF)

9. In general, mountainous regions do **not** support any population clusters, and never have. (TF)

10. Industries could be found in different parts of the world 6000 years ago. (TF)

STUDY QUESTIONS

1. When you read about the Pleistocene epoch can you understand the environmental problems our human ancestors faced? Can you understand why some branches of the early human family tree died out?

2. Why is the Holocene epoch different from previous epochs? List the accomplishments of humankind during this period and contrast it to previous periods. What do you think might happen when Earth goes into another ice age? How might people survive?

3. Explain what caused the changes in early settlement. How was the social structure changed? Was this change uniform among the settlements?

4. Why do geographers consider Köppen's climate classifications so important? Compare text Figure 3-5 (World Climates) with text Figure 20-1 (World Agriculture Regions). What correlations can you find between climate and crops grown? How can you tell from the climate map where people are most likely to live?

Notes

Notes

PART TWO: POPULATION PATTERNS AND PROCESSES

CHAPTER 4.   FUNDAMENTALS OF POPULATION: LOCATION, DISTRIBUTION, AND DENSITY

CHAPTER INTRODUCTION

No event in human history has equaled the rapid increase in population over the last 10,000 years. This is in sharp contrast to the 200,000 years following the emergence of *Homo sapiens* in Africa, during which the earth's human population grew very slowly, its numbers rising and falling in response to the "traditional" controllers of population: environmental change, disease, and availability of food. As the last glaciation retreated and the Holocene epoch began, the amount of habitable space increased and unprecedented events began to occur in Earth's history.

The study of population is termed *demography,* derived from ancient Greek words roughly meaning to "describe and write about people." The focus of *population geography* is on the spatial aspects of demography. The key questions in geography are *where* and *why there?* These lead to some penetrating insights into population issues.

Population Growth

The dominant issue in population geography remains *growth*. The world's population is currently growing at a rate that is more than ten times the *total* estimated world population at the beginning of the Holocene and the bulk of this growth is occurring in the world's poorer countries. The Earth's environments and natural resources are strained as never before by the needs of a mushrooming human population, a population that has more than doubled in the last 50 years. Problems resulting from unprecedented population growth became especially acute in the twentieth century. A continued high rate of population growth in the twenty-first century can have a calamitous impact, causing irreversible damage to the natural systems on which we depend for our existence and survival.

Population Distribution

From the beginning, humanity has been unevenly distributed over the land and this pattern was intensified during the twentieth century. Whether urban or rural, populations tend to cluster in certain areas (see text Figure 4-1) because, as you will recall from earlier discussions, much of the Earth is unsuitable for human occupancy (refer back to text figures 3-4 and 3-5). To handle contrasts of this type on maps, geographers use measures of population *distribution*—the locations on the Earth's surface where individuals or groups (depending on the scale of the map) are concentrated —and the *density* of the population figured as the number of people per unit area of land.

Text Figure 4-1 shows patterns of population distribution for the world using the dot method. It shows that the world's three largest population concentrations all lie on the Eurasian landmass —*East Asia*, *South Asia*, and *Europe*—each associated with a major civilization. It also reminds us that the overwhelming majority of the world's population inhabits the Northern Hemisphere.

East Asia, centered on China but extending to Korea and Japan, contains about one-quarter of the world's population—nearly 1.3 billion in China alone. The map shows that the population is concentrated toward the coast with ribbon-like extensions found on the basins and lowlands of China's major rivers. The great majority of people in East Asia are farmers.

India lies at the center of the South Asian concentration with extensions to Pakistan, Bangladesh, and the island of Sri Lanka. This is one of the greatest concentrations of people on Earth with about 1.5 billion people. It is a confined region (the Himalaya Mountains on the north and the desert west of the Indus River in Pakistan) with a rapidly growing population. By almost any estimate, the capacity of the region to support this population has been exceeded. As in East Asia, the majority are farmers.

Europe, the third-ranking population cluster, also lies in Eurasia but at the opposite end from China. This cluster contains about 700 million people, which puts it in a class with the South Asian concentration, but the similarity ends there. In Europe, unlike East and South Asia, terrain and environment are not as closely related to population distribution. Another contrast lies in the fact that the majority of the European population live in cities and towns, leaving the rural countryside more open and sparsely populated. These contrasts with the East and South Asian clusters reflect the impact of the Industrial Revolution on Europe over the last 200-plus years.

Population Density

Population density can be measured on the basis of several different criteria, revealing contrasting aspects of a country's demography. Text Figure 4-2 illustrates density via the isopleth method. The data in Resource B at the end of your textbook provide area, total population, and density per square mile for every country. One must examine such data with caution, however, since the high cost and organizational challenges of census taking often produce unreliable data. *Arithmetic* and *physiologic* population densities are the two most common approaches. These two methods become more meaningful and useful when compared with each other.

CHAPTER QUIZ

MULTIPLE-CHOICE QUESTIONS

1. Demography is the study of:
   a. physical geography
   b. population
   c. animals
   d. climate

2. Which country has the highest arithmetic density of people.
   a. Japan
   b. Bangladesh
   c. India
   d. Netherlands

3. Physiologic density of a country relates the total population of a country to the:
   a. number of people living on farmlands
   b. population divided into total acres of farmland

c. acres of farmland available

d. population living in villages and cities

4. About __?__ of the world's population lives in East Asia.
   a. one-half
   b. one-third
   c. one-fifth
   d. one-fourth

5. One of the greatest concentrations of population, according to your text, is:
   a. in Argentina
   b. on the Ganges River plain in northern India
   c. in Bangladesh
   d. on the Nile River

6. In Germany __?__ percent of the people live in cities.
   a. 85
   b. 90
   c. 50
   d. 75

7. In the United States, the largest urban complex, called a megalopolis, lies:
   a. in Florida and north to South Carolina
   b. along the Pacific coast in Southern California
   c. in Chicago and its surrounding area
   d. from Boston to Baltimore

8. Southeast Asia has __?__ clusters of population.
   a. contiguous
   b. few
   c. discrete
   d. large

9. The population of Sub-Saharan Africa is nearly:
   a. 200 million
   b. 350 million
   c. 400 million
   d. 650 million

10. Geographically, the spatial distribution of population in Australia and South America is:
    a. very scattered
    b. concentrated in the interior regions
    c. peripheral
    d. concentrated on plateaus

TRUE/FALSE QUESTIONS

1. In the poorer countries, people tend to cluster in the urban areas because there is little farmland. (TF)

2. Population distribution dot-maps are used primarily to show where people live. (TF)

3. Physiologic density maps more accurately show population densities because they are based on urban land clusters. (TF)

4. In China, farmers far outnumber people living in cities. (TF)

5. The country of Bangladesh has a population of nearly 133 million people living in an area about the size of Iowa. (TF)

6. In contrast to East and South Asia, Europe's population centers are not closely related to terrain and environment. Instead they are related exclusively to the coal-fields. (TF)

7. In the United States the largest urban agglomeration is located along the Pacific coast. (TF)

8. Southeast Asia does not have large contiguous urban areas because it is made up of islands. (TF)

9. In Africa, there are no agglomerations comparable to those in Asia. (TF)

10. With land reforms it would be possible for South America to support a much larger population. (TF)

STUDY QUESTIONS

1. List and explain the problems high population growth rates are causing in the world today.

2. Define and discuss the difference between arithmetic and physiologic densities. What is lacking in each? Why aren't either of these completely accurate?

3. How does the spatial distribution of population of North America and Europe differ from that of East Asia and South Asia? How are populations spatially distributed in South America and Australia?

4. How does Japan support its large population? What special problems does this country have that are not faced by the other developed nations?

Notes

Notes

CHAPTER 5. PROCESSES AND CYCLES OF POPULATION CHANGE

CHAPTER INTRODUCTION

Population does not increase in an even manner from country to country. The differences include age, gender, life expectancy, and geographic distribution, and may be identified between countries but are more significant internally. A country that has a large percentage of its population at 15 years of age or below will have enormous needs for education, jobs, and housing in the years ahead. A country where the population is "aging," such as the United States or France, can face shortages of younger workers and problems with their retirement systems. The list goes on but you get the point: a population is far more than mere numbers. This is an extremely important chapter, and when you have studied it, you will have a much better understanding of the complex issues of world population.

Population Trends
Never before in human history have so many people filled the Earth's living space, and never has world population grown as rapidly as it has during the past 100 years. The population explosion of the past 200 years has increased the world's population from under 1 billion to approximately 6 billion. It took from the dawn of history to the year 1820 for the Earth's population to reach 1 billion. It now is taking only a decade to add each new billion. It is still possible that there will be 10 billion human inhabitants on the planet by the middle of the twenty-first century.

Population Growth Rates
Rapid population growth varies over time and space. Europe's rapid growth occurred during the nineteenth century, the result of the Second Agricultural Revolution. At this time better farming methods and improved organization resulted in increased food supplies, especially to cities and towns. This was immediately followed by the Industrial Revolution, during which sanitation facilities made the towns and cities safer from epidemics, and modern medical practices became wide spread. Disease prevention through vaccination introduced a new era in public health. Death rates declined markedly—by 50 percent between 1750 and 1850—while birth rates remained high. The change is especially spectacular when viewed in the context of doubling time—the number of years it takes a population to double—which was 150 years in 1750 but only 35 years in 1850.

One effect of this increase in the rate of natural population growth was increased migration. Millions of people left Europe to emigrate to other parts of the world—North and South America, Australia, South Africa, and elsewhere. When European colonization began in earnest during the nineteenth century, Europeans brought with them their newfound methods of sanitation and medical techniques and death rates in Africa, India, and South America began to decline. Indigenous populations began to grow, and at ever-increasing rates. Today, South America's growth rates have declined, but Africa's remain high. As mentioned previously, the fastest-growing populations today are invariably taking place in those poorer countries that have the greatest difficulties providing the basic amenities of life for their citizens.

Disease and famine were the major controllers of population for the world as a whole until the last 100 years. Diseases still kill millions of people each year, especially infants and children, but the overall effects have been reduced, at least in many countries.

25

Reduction of Growth Rates

Reducing population growth rates is a complicated and sensitive issue. In the richer, more developed countries, general modernization and education has resulted in lower growth rates. Therefore, these countries total populations do not approach those of the poorer countries. The benefits enjoyed by the wealthier, developed nations that have led to their slower rates of population have not been shared by much of the world. A key issue to the reduction of population growth rates is to improve the status of women and to secure their rights in society. In the Muslim countries of Southwest Asia and Sub-Saharan Africa, two of the regions with the highest rates of population growth, women often live in near-Medieval conditions or, at best, as second-class citizens. Tradition plays a powerful role, but the barrier to better education for women is the real key. In places where women's education levels have risen, there has been an accompanying decline in population growth rates; not to mention a general improvement in the well-being of the population.

The demographic transition model, which compares birth and death rates in a population over time, suggests that the world's population will stabilize in the twenty-first century, but the model may not be universally applicable. The sequence of stages of the demographic transition has been observed in several European countries, but what transpired economically and socially in Europe may not apply for the rest of the world. It may be unwise, therefore, to assume that the demographic cycles that have occurred in already-industrialized countries will eventually spread to the rest of the world.

CHAPTER QUIZ

MULTIPLE-CHOICE QUESTIONS

1. At the present time, about __?__ million people are added to the world's population each year.
   a. 150
   b. 100
   c. 90
   d. 80

2. Today, Russia is experiencing a __?__ population growth rate.
   a. rising
   b. declining
   c. negative
   d. stable

3. Africa's rate of natural increase in population is still high but its population faces the grim prospects of:
   a. a decade or more of drought
   b. increasing ethnic strife in all countries
   c. the AIDS epidemic
   d. increasing military conflict

4. The continent with the lowest birth rates is:
   a. Europe
   b. North America

c. Southeast Asia

d. Antarctica

5. The total fertility rate of a country measures the total number of:
   a. women able to have children
   b. children between 1 year old and age 10
   c. women between 13 and 45
   d. children born to women of childbearing age

6. Crude death rates are highest in:
   a. tropical Africa
   b. China
   c. South Africa
   d. South America

7. Which of the following did **not** have an effect on keeping population growth rates down before 1820.
   a. the Little Ice Age
   b. wars
   c. plagues
   d. advances in medicine

8. The actual demographic transition is represented by which two of the four stages of the demographic transition model.
   a. 1 and 4
   b. 2 and 3
   c. 3 and 4
   d. 2 and 4

9. It is thought by some that perhaps today's developing countries will __?__ of the demographic transition model.
   a. not go through all four stages
   b. have to go through all four stages
   c. not follow any stages
   d. only go through stages two and three

10. As a tool for development, the demographic transition model is most useful in one place.
    a. United States
    b. Europe
    c. Japan
    d. Canada

TRUE/FALSE QUESTIONS

1. Because of the world's falling population growth rate, there is no longer fear of a population explosion. (TF)

2. Population growth rates are rising in the Muslim countries of North Africa and Southwest Asia. (TF)

3. Not all of the countries with low birth rates are wealthy. (TF)

4. Thomas Malthus thought the world's population growth would be slowed by disease. (TF)

5. By 2030, people in Germany over age 65 will account for close to half the adult population. (TF)

6. Population geography is the spatial component of demography. (TF)

7. Japan's population is projected to begin expanding rapidly in 2007. (TF)

8. Crude death rates decline more rapidly than birth rates. (TF)

9. In Between 1348 and 1350, almost half the population of England died from bubonic plague. (TF)

10. Most countries in the world are at the same stage of the demographic transition model. (TF)

STUDY QUESTIONS

1. Look at text Figure 5-1. Note where the high population growth rate countries are. Do you see a pattern?

2. Even though the world's overall population growth rate has slowed, why is there still concern about another population explosion? Explain exponential growth and why the base population is so important worldwide and by country. Use text Figure 5-2 to help you. What kinds of problems can you foresee for those countries that have a high rate of growth today?

3. Study text Figures 5-4 and 5-5. Explain what you can learn by looking at these age-sex pyramids.

4. Study the section under the heading Demographic Cycles. Write down all the terms and their definitions in this section.

5. After studying the demographic cycle, do you understand why the four stages might not apply to today's developing countries? How did European colonization affect these countries?

Notes

Notes

CHAPTER 6.   WHERE AND WHY PEOPLE MOVE

CHAPTER INTRODUCTION

Humans have always been mobile. Throughout history humans have sought new frontiers and the search still continues today. For more than 90 percent of human history there were hunter-gatherers, a practice that required frequent relocation. Such movement is called *migration*, and while the reasons for such movement are different today, human mobility has actually increased in modern times.

Human mobility is of central interest in human geography because it is an inherently spatial process. Human movement speeds the diffusion of ideas and innovations. It intensifies spatial interaction and transforms whole regions. And as you will see in this chapter, it is often closely linked to environmental conditions.

Why People Move
Many factors stimulate the migration process. They include armed conflict, economic conditions (real or perceived), political strife, cultural circumstances (such as linguistic or religious differences), environmental change (growing more common today), and technological advances (which makes information about destinations more easily obtainable and movement easier). Migration today occurs for various other reasons but those listed are the principle ones.

Migrants move on the basis of their perceptions of particular destinations, taking into consideration both direction and distance. Direction, like location, can be viewed in two ways: *absolute* and *relative*. Absolute direction refers to astronomically determined direction and thus is what we think of as *compass* direction. Relative direction is more perceptual and often imprecise, as in the case of the Sunbelt. The residents of North Dakota, for example, would agree that Florida lies to the south and is part of the Sunbelt, but not everyone would agree that Utah is also. Different people have different perceptions.

Distance, like direction, can be measured in both absolute and relative terms. *Absolute distance* is the physical distance between two points usually using kilometers or miles; it can be read on maps using the scale of the map. Absolute distance does not change. *Relative distance*—measured not in linear terms such as miles or kilometers, but in terms such as cost or time—has different meanings for different people and cultures. It can change due to, say, a new method of transportation or the discovery of a shorter route. Research has shown that people's perception of both distance and direction can be greatly distorted, and that distance particularly affects the accuracy of migrants perception of their destinations.

Forms of Human Mobility
Mobility of all kinds is one of the defining characteristics of a culture. The great majority of people have a daily routine that takes them through a sequence of short moves that geographers call *activity (or action) space*. The magnitude of activity space varies in different societies, and American society is the world's most mobile. Technology has greatly expanded activity space, particularly in the wealthier, more developed countries.

There are three general types of movement recognized by geographers and others who study human mobility. *Cyclic movement*—movement that has a closed route—defines your activity space. When you go to daily classes or a job you are participating in cyclic movement. If your trip involves a lengthy period of residency after your arrival—such as temporary relocation for college attendance or service in the armed services—you are engaged in *periodic movement*. Both types of movement occur in many forms. Finally, *migratory movement* describes human movement from a source to a destination without a return journey, and is the most significant form of movement discussed in this chapter. A society's mobility is measured as the sum of cyclic, periodic, and migratory movement of its population.

Factors of Migration

The decision to migrate usually results from a combination of conditions and perceptions that tend to induce people to leave their abodes. Geographers who study human migration call the negative conditions and perceptions *push factors*. The positive conditions and perceptions that effectively attract people to a new locale from other areas are called *pull factors*. Push factors are likely to be perceived more accurately than pull factors, since people are more likely to be familiar with their place of residence (source) than the locale to which they are moving. Push factors include individual considerations ranging from work or retirement conditions to weather and climate. Pull factors tend to be more vague and many migrants move on the basis of excessively positive images and expectations regarding their destinations.

Our final look at the reasons people move focuses on the luxury of choice and the fear of compulsion. These may be classed as *voluntary* and *forced migrations*. There are different cases within each of these categories and it is not always easy to make a clear determination. In the case of the millions of Europeans who came to the Americas, most were seeking opportunity and better living conditions. These same motives carried others far from Europe to African and Asian colonies. The prevailing force was the "pull" of opportunity and thus, for the most part, emigrants from Europe left by choice.

Several of the world's largest migration streams have been forced migrations, which result from the imposition of power by stronger peoples over weaker ones. By far the most important of these was the Transatlantic *slave trade*, which carried tens of millions of Africans from their homes to the Americas, with enormous loss of life. From 12 million to over 30 million Africans were sold into slavery (see text Figure 6-3) and nothing in human history compares to the Atlantic slave trade. Both source and destination regions were affected, with the African sources being socially and demographically devastated for generations. Forced countermigration continues today when governments send back migrants caught entering their countries illegally.

CHAPTER QUIZ

MULTIPLE-CHOICE QUESTIONS

1. Which country has the most mobile population.
   a. England
   b. United States
   c. France
   d. Ireland

2. Emigration occurs when a person:
   a. moves from their home country
   b. relocates to another part of their own country
   c. enters a new country as a migrant
   d. moves to another location in the same town

3. During the 1990s, legal migration from Mexico exceeded:
   a. 500,000
   b. 750,000
   c. 1 million
   d. 2.5 million

4. In the last few centuries, which of the following source areas has had the most voluntary emigrants.
   a. Africa
   b. South Asia
   c. Europe
   d. the Caribbean

5. For 50 years beginning in 1788, tens of thousands of convicts were shipped from Britain to:
   a. South Africa
   b. North America
   c. South America
   d. Australia

6. Which of the following is a special form of periodic movement.
   a. transhumance
   b. migrant labor
   c. nomadism
   d. commuting

7. During the forced migration of Africans in the sixteenth century, slaves were first brought to:
   a. Central America
   b. the United States
   c. the Caribbean
   d. Brazil

8. Which group of people suffered the worst as refugees after the Gulf War in 1991.
   a. Iranians
   b. Kurds
   c. Palestinians
   d. Saudis

9. In 1997, which Western Hemisphere country had a serious refugee problem that was drug related.
   a. Columbia
   b. Mexico
   c. Haiti
   d. Cuba

10 During the last decade of the twentieth century and the first years of the twenty-first, the world's largest refugee crisis prevailed in:
    a. Southwest Asia
    b. South America
    c. Europe
    d. Sub-Saharan Africa

TRUE/FALSE QUESTIONS

1. Absolute distance is actually the same as relative distance. (TF)

2. People's perception of distance is actually quite accurate. (TF)

3. The term *internal migration* is how geographers describe the migration of black families that moved from the South to the North in the United States. (TF)

4. Economic conditions have not been a major reason for emigration. (TF)

5. The decision to migrate usually results from a combination of push and pull factors. (TF)

6. Because of distance decay, many migrants move in what is called step migration. (TF)

7. Both voluntary and forced migration generate a return, or counter, migration. (TF)

8. Even before Cuba became a communist state, thousands of Cuban citizens annually applied for residency in the United States. (TF)

9. During Afghanistan's war with the former Soviet Union, there were no international refugees because the Soviets surrounded the country. (TF)

10. In forecasting the future, experts believe the refugee problem will lessen and probably disappear. (TF)

STUDY QUESTIONS

1. Describe external and internal migration. What is the difference? How has internal migration affected the great urban areas of the United States?

2. List and define the factors that make people migrate. How do push/pull factors come into play? Read Ravenstein's "laws" of migration carefully and apply them to migrations given as examples in this chapter.

3. List the differences between voluntary and forced migration.

4. List the three characteristics that distinguish refugees from migrants. Can you describe situations that might create intranational refugees? Describe situations that have created refugee crises in Africa.

Notes

Notes

CHAPTER 7.   POLICY RESPONSES TO DEMOGRAPHIC CHANGES

CHAPTER INTRODUCTION

Since humans first set foot on the Earth they have continually engaged in movement and increased in numbers. Thousands of years ago this was not the problem it is today for several reasons. The numbers of humans were far fewer than exist today and humanity then engaged in a hunting and gathering existence, which required considerably movement. Mobility was an accepted part of life. Add to this the complete lack of any political or geographic organization (what we call countries today), and because there were no political borders, which today restrict movement, many of the problems facing humanity toady were absent.

Today humanity faces a more important factor that has developed over the last few centuries —a high degree of mobility. Whereas early humans existed in homogeneous groups that were far more isolated from others, this is not the case today, so that tolerance of differences between different people and cultures was not the pressing issue that it is in the twenty-first century. Add to this the enormous increases in human numbers, essentially crowded into the same areas of the Earth's surface as they were hundreds of years ago with a wide range of differences in political and cultural attitudes and values, and you begin to see the problems faced by those charged with developing policies and guidelines for demographic questions.

National Population Policies
Population policies in the twenty-first century must be considered in both a temporal as well as a spatial context. These two issues are critical but far from separate because much has changed in the world since the sixteenth century when the age of global exploration and discovery would result in the spread of different cultures across the face of the Earth. This process resulted in the end of cultural isolation, particularly in the twentieth century, and presented societies and governments with problems never before faced.

Consider also that the issues of demographic change must be considered by governments in both an international and intranational context. In many countries today, immigrants account for as many, if not more, new citizens than do indigenous births. Such movement has impacts on both the source regions and destinations, and the reaction of residents in the latter often create further problems.

Controlling Migration
Migration control and its attendant problems have become hot issues around the world. Efforts to restrict migrations are nothing new; media coverage, democratic debate, and political wrangling only make it seem so. China's Great Wall was built in part as a barrier to emigration, as were the Berlin Wall and the fences along the Rio Grande—all evidence of the desire of governments to control the movement of people across their borders. Physical as well as legal barriers are placed in the way of migrants, but few countries have succeeded in effectively controlling immigration effectively, or without controversy.

CHAPTER QUIZ

MULTIPLE-CHOICE QUESTIONS

1. The United Nations holds population conferences every __?__ years.
   a. 5
   b. 10
   c. 2
   d. when necessary

2. When women have access to education and paid employment, birth rates in a country or region:
   a. go up
   b. remain the same
   c. go down
   d. cause women to remain single and support themselves

3. The United States National Origins Law was passed in:
   a. 1929
   b. 1939
   c. 1909
   d. 1979

4. Which of the following is **not** true about Japan's efforts to increase productivity in an aging population.
   a. government is giving benefits to families encouraging them to have more children
   b. couples are discouraged because of the high cost of raising children
   c. technology will provide increased productivity
   d. the importation of foreign workers

5. The first immigration laws in the United States were passed in:
   a. 1877
   b. 1882
   c. 1912
   d. 1917

6. Today, some countries are pushing expansive population policies because:
   a. their populations are aging and declining
   b. they want to better balance the gender ratio of their population
   c. this policy was encouraged by all countries attending the Cairo conference
   d. With the availability of modern technology, large families are now cheaper

7. Which of the following countries is given as an example of the fact that many governments have learned that changing circumstances tend to overtake carefully constructed population policies.
   a. United States
   b. Germany
   c. Singapore
   d. Australia

8 Which of the following countries has the most successful family-planning programs in the Muslim world.
   a. Saudi Arabia
   b. Indonesia
   c. Iran
   d. Egypt

9 Demographers predict that this country, sometime during the first half of this twenty-first century, will surpass China as the world's most populous country.
   a. Indonesia
   b. Russia
   c. Brazil
   d. India

10. This country's one-child policy of the past has resulted in a major social impact where, in the
    future males will greatly outnumber females within the population.
    a. China
    b. India
    c. Japan
    d. Indonesia

TRUE/FALSE QUESTIONS

1. Efforts by countries to restrict all types of immigration are a relatively new development. (TF)

2. China's one-child policy has caused no long-range problems for its population development. (TF)

3. In 1948 the government of India passed the Eugenic Protection Act. (TF)

4. The country of Saudi Arabia is at the heart of the Muslim world. (TF)

5. The natural rate of population increase is at its lowest in the heart of the Roman Catholic world. (TF)

6. At the beginning of the twenty-first century the world's population "bomb" is defused. (TF)

7. The Great Wall of China was built to control both emigration and immigration. (TF)

8. At the first UN Population Conference, China was in favor of population control. (TF)

9. Australia's immigration law of 1901 was passed to keep out all nonwhite immigrants. (TF)

10. Many countries have passed immigration laws restricting persons of different ethnic backgrounds. (TF)

STUDY QUESTIONS

1. Discuss in chronological order the various policy changes to control population growth that have been undertaken by the government of communist China.

2. India was one of the first so-called developing countries to institute population planning in the 1950s. Discuss some of the measures that were taken and the problems encountered. Why may it be impossible for a country like India to develop programs and policies that are acceptable to its citizens?

3. At the UN Population Control meetings, countries have differing opinions. Discuss these opinions and each country's objections. How does this affect efforts to control worldwide population growth?

4. Over the years, what different measures have countries taken to restrict immigration? Toward which ethnic groups were these measures aimed?

Notes

Notes

PART THREE: THE GLOBAL LINGUISTIC MOSAIC

CHAPTER 8.   A GEOGRAPHY OF LANGUAGES

CHAPTER INTRODUCTION

Language is one of the cornerstones of national identity, cultural unity, and community cohesion. It is the most important *cultural glue*—an aspect that binds a culture together—because without language, there would be no culture. People have very strong feelings about their language and identify with it (people may be persuaded to change their religion much more easily than their language). When a people's language is threatened, the response is often passionate and protective.

Thousands of languages are spoken in the world today (linguists estimate between 5000 and 6000), and they serve as both unifiers and dividers of humanity. Ironically, all languages may have a common origin. Consider the following points carefully as you read this chapter.

Standard Language
Human languages, even those spoken in preliterate societies—people who speak their language but do not write it—are fundamentally different from those of nonhuman primates. Human languages are not static but change constantly because a vital culture requires a flexible language and the potential vocabulary of any language is infinite.

Mature and complex cultures—technologically advanced societies—attempt to maintain a *standard language* sustained by national institutions and official state examinations. In the modern world, where innovations diffuse rapidly, such standards are difficult to uphold. One problem that arises is: who decides what the standard language will be? Not surprisingly, the answer has to do with influence and power—circumstances that often produce problems in a world where cultural identity and national self-interest are increasingly significant.

Classification and Distribution of Languages
The problem of language classification relates to the definition of language. At issue is what is a language (according to the dictionary: "human communication by voice") and what is a dialect ("language of a particular area or class")? The issue is a complex one and it is clear that the distinction is not based on an objective measure of mutual intelligibility. Instead, it must be recognized that what we consider a language is a function of society's view of what constitutes a cultural community—a matter that in turn is influenced by historical development in the political arena.

Language classification uses terms that are also employed in biology, and for the same reasons: some languages are related and some are not. *Language families* are thought to have a shared, but fairly distant, origin; in a *language subfamily*, the commonality is more definite. Subfamilies are divided into *language groups*, which consist of sets of individual languages.

Text Figure 8-2 shows the distribution of 20 major language families. On this map, only the Indo-European language family is broken down into subfamilies (greater detail is shown in text Figure 8-3). Spatially, the Indo-European languages are the most widely dispersed. More people speak languages belonging to the Indo-European language family than those in any other family. There are good reasons for this pattern. When the European migration of emigrants and colonists spread over the world in the last 500 years, one of the cultural components that spread with them was their languages. Add to this the fact that indigenous populations were virtually wiped out in the Americas and Australia (and their languages with them) and the European desire to spread the Christian faith, usually in the language of the European culture invading the area, and the patterns on the map become easier to understand.

Major World Languages

Chinese is spoken by more people than any other language (Table 8-1), with English ranking second. The numbers in Table 8-1, however, should be viewed as approximations only. English is the primary language of 350 million people in 6 major countries and numerous smaller countries with millions of inhabitants; it is also used as a second language of hundreds of millions in India, Africa, and elsewhere. English has also become the principal language of cross-culture communications, economics, and science. In a world where rapid communication and travel is becoming more the norm than the exception, this has some benefits, since there is no such thing as a "global language," at least not officially. Consider, for example, the possible problems on an international airline trip if the cockpit crew spoke one language and the airport control tower personnel another. Fortunately, there is supposed to be an English-speaking person in each location. English is also spreading with the World Wide Web, at least to countries where there is access.

The present distribution of languages, as revealed on maps, is useful in understanding cultural development and change. Text Figure 8-4, for example, indicates the four Dravidian languages are all spoken in a compact region in the south of the Indian Peninsula. The map thus suggests these languages (which are older) and the cultures they represent were "pushed" southward by the advancing Indo-European speakers. Similar interesting patterns can be observed in text Figure 8-3 by looking at the spatial pattern of the Germanic and Romance language subfamilies.

CHAPTER QUIZ

MULTIPLE-CHOICE QUESTIONS

1. A group of people who speak a language but have no written form of it, are said to be:
   a. illiterate
   b. prehistoric
   c. preliterate
   d. symbolic

2. All languages have at least one thing in common they:
   a. change over time
   b. remain static
   c. do not borrow from other languages
   d. do not use symbols

3. Africa has more than __?__ spoken languages.
   a. 500
   b. 1000
   c. 1200
   d. 1500

4. Spatially the __?__ language family is the most widely dispersed.
    a. Afro-Asiatic
    b. Ural-Altaic
    c. Indo-European
    d. Khoisan

5. Latin was spread over Europe by the:
    a. Muslims
    b. Greeks
    c. Romans
    d. English

6. The language family in Sub-Saharan Africa with the most speakers is:
    a. Afro-Asiatic
    b. Niger-Congo
    c. Khoisan
    d. Indo-European

7. In India which Dravidian language has the most speakers.
    a. Telugu
    b. Tamil
    c. Kanarese
    d. Malayalam

8. The oldest language family in Sub-Saharan Africa is the __?__ .
    a. Sudanic
    b. Afro-Asiatic
    c. Indo-European
    d. Khoisan

9. The language spoken by more Chinese than any other is:
    a. Mandarin
    b. Wu
    c. Cantonese
    d. Gung Ho

10. In British Hong Kong the language most often spoken was:
    a. Mandarin
    b. Cantonese
    c. English
    d. Japanese

TRUE/FALSE QUESTIONS

1. Today all of the world's languages are being preserved and will continue to be spoken. (TF)

2. Linguists estimate between 2000 and 3000 languages are being spoken in the world today. (TF)

3. In today's world, because of migration, most developed countries do **not** have a standard language. (TF)

4. Thanks to the English colonial masters, India has only about 100 different languages. (TF)

5. Native American languages do **not** remain strong in the United States. (TF)

6. In Europe, the Basque language is spoken in a very small area. (TF)

7. India has hundreds of languages, most of which are spoken by few people. (TF)

8. Close to 1000 languages in Africa are unwritten. (TF)

9. An isogloss is a geographic boundary within which a particular linguistic feature occurs. (TF)

10. Speakers of the three major dialects of the Chinese language can easily understand each other. (TF)

STUDY QUESTIONS

1. What are the major components that make up the definition of language as spoken by humans? What is a standard language? How does the text explain a dialect and isoglosses?

2. Look at text Figures 8-2 and 8-3. What does this tell you about the spread of the Indo-European languages? How do you think colonialism and migration (ancient and recent) helped in spreading these languages?

3. In text Figure 8-5 we can see the location of Africa's language families. How does the text explain their location? How are different subfamilies related? Why is the Khoisan family considered the oldest?

4. Why is there debate over whether Chinese is one or several languages?

Notes

Notes

CHAPTER 9.   THE DIFFUSION OF LANGUAGES

CHAPTER INTRODUCTION

Understanding the origin and diffusion of languages is essential to understanding the diffusion of humanity. By understanding where and how languages developed, we learn about the people who spoke them. Although there is disagreement on when language arose, there is no question that it was vital to the development of humanity. By studying the development and changes in languages we learn much about the development of humans and their cultures.

Language Origins

The search for the origins of language goes back tens of thousands of years. It has yielded information not only about how language changes but also about the environments where early languages were spoken. Linguistic reconstruction methods are still controversial, but with the help of computers, remarkable progress is being made in the reconstruction of ancient languages and their paths of diffusion.

The diversification of languages has long been charted through the analysis of *sound shifts* —finding similar words with the same meaning in different languages and determining their common language of origin. If it is possible to deduce a large part of the vocabulary of an extinct language, it may be possible to recreate the language that preceded it. This technique, called *deep reconstruction,* has yielded some important results. It takes humanity's linguistic family tree back thousands of years.

Scientists do not yet agree on how long ago language emerged. Some believe that the use of language began with the rise of *Homo sapiens* 200,000 or more years ago; others argue that simple vocal communication began much earlier.

The first major linguistic hypothesis proposed the existence of an ancestral *Proto-Indo-European* language (or closely related languages) as the predecessor of Latin, Greek, and Sanskrit, among other ancient languages. The proposed ancestral language(s) would link not only the romance languages but also a number of other languages spoken from Britain to North Africa and South Asia.

The Language Tree

In the mid-nineteenth century August Schleicher, a German linguist, compared the world's language families to the branches of a tree. He suggested that the basic process of language formation is *language divergence*—differentiation over time and space. Languages would branch into dialects; isolation then increased the differences between dialects. Over time, dialects would become discrete languages. Schleicher's idea has stood the test of time and criticism, and the language-tree model remains central to language research (text Figure 9-1).

A complicating factor is that with human mobility, languages did not merely diffuse through static populations; they also spread by relocation diffusion (see Chapter 2). If this caused long-isolated languages to make contact, *language convergence* occurred. Researchers then face special problems because the rules of reconstruction may or may not apply.

Modern cultural events add a further complication. We know that the languages of traditional, numerically smaller, and technologically less advanced people have been replaced, or greatly modified, by the languages of invaders. This process of *language replacement* goes on today, and there is every reason to believe that it has happened ever since humans began to use language. Thus languages change through divergence, convergence, and replacement, making the spatial search for origins problematic.

49

Recent Language Diffusion

The final stages of the dispersal of the older languages—before the global diffusion of English and other Indo-European languages—occurred in the Pacific realm and in the Americas. One would thus assume that the historical geography of these events would be easier to reconstruct than the complex situation in western Eurasia, but this is not the case. While the relatively recent spread of languages to these two realms does provide useful information for the reconstruction of language diffusion routes and processes, an examination of the debates over Pacific and American native languages reveals that the problems are not simple at all.

Much remains to be learned about the reasons behind the complexity of the Pacific language map, to say nothing about the debate over human migration to, and language development and dif-fusion in, the Americas. One theory holds that there were three waves of early human migration to the Americas from Asia producing three families of indigenous American languages. A majority of linguists still doubt the three-wave hypothesis and the three-family map of American languages. Genetic research and archeological studies will ultimately solve the issue. In the meantime, we are reminded of the gaps still remaining in our knowledge.

Influences on Individual Languages

Each of the languages in the world's language families has its own story of origin and dispersal. It is clear, however, that there are certain critical influences on the diffusion of individual tongues. First, speakers of nonwritten languages will not retain the same language very long if they lose contact with one another. Second, the diffusion of a single tongue over a large area occurs only when people remain in contact with one another and continue to rely on a common linguistic frame of reference. Three critical components therefore have influenced the world's linguistic mosaic: writing, technology, and political organization.

CHAPTER QUIZ

MULTIPLE-CHOICE QUESTIONS

1. The use of sound shifts helps trace languages back toward their origins. This technique is called:
   a. backward reconstruction
   b. root tracing
   c. deep reconstruction
   d. language foundation tracing

2. When the most wide-spread language family was studied backward, it is believed this family came from a language we now call:
   a. the mother tongue
   b. the ancestral language
   c. Proto-Indo-European
   d. Proto-Anatolian

3. In tracing languages backward many factors must be taken into consideration, such as:
   a. language convergence
   b. the replacement of language by invading forces
   c. linguistic islands
   d. all of the above

4. A pre-Proto-Indo-European language called Nostratic, and researched independently by two Russian researchers, was based on words for:
   a. body parts and elements of the natural environment
   b. landforms and climate
   c. tools and utensils
   d. domesticated plants

5. In which of the following world regions did the last diffusion of the older languages take place.
   a. the Indian Ocean
   b. the Pacific and Americas
   c. the South Atlantic
   d. Central Asia

6. The diffusion of peoples and their languages into the Pacific north of Indonesia traces its roots to which of the following.
   a. coastal New Guinea
   b. coastal India
   c. coastal China
   d. coastal Australia

7. The current language map of the Americas is dominated by:
   a. Native American languages
   b. Austronesian languages
   c. Malayo-Polynesian languages
   d. Indo-European languages

8. As many as 40 language families have been recognized in the Old World, but linguists have identified as many as __?__ Native American language families in the Americas.
   a. 100
   b. 200
   c. 300
   d. 400

9. The world's linguistic mosaic has been influenced by three critical components. Which of the following is **not** one of these.
   a. transportation
   b. writing
   c. technology
   d. political organization

10. The development of the printing press in the late Middle Ages had an enormous influence on the development of the standard form of basic languages through the availability of printed texts. What was the subject of many of these early texts.
    a. commerce
    b. literature
    c. religion
    d. science

TRUE/FALSE QUESTIONS

1. The languages of Greek, Latin, and Sanskrit are related. (TF)

2. Occurring only in the past, language replacement occurred when invaders took over a small weaker group. (TF)

3. Those who believe the agriculture theory of language diffusion think the first language diffused from the Fertile Crescent. (TF)

4. The diffusion of people and their languages into the Pacific north of Indonesia and New Guinea began in China. (TF)

5. In the Western Hemisphere, as many as 200 Native American languages families have been identified. (TF)

6. The theory that North America's first immigrants arrived about 12,000 years ago has not been challenged. (TF)

7. Having a written language allows that language to become stabilized. (TF)

8. Because many early printed texts were religious they changed the way people spoke. (TF)

9. When early large political systems collapsed, language divergence took place. (TF)

10. Language can either bring people together or cause conflict. (TF)

STUDY QUESTIONS

1. Describe the process of deep reconstruction and the role of sound shifts. What factors create problems for people trying to reconstruct old languages?

2. Discuss the theories of language diffusion. How does Renfrew carry one of these further?

3. By looking at text Figure 9-6, and reading the text, follow the diffusion of language in the Pacific. Discuss problems encountered in interpreting the time frame and number of migrations.

4. Discuss controversies surrounding the diffusion of languages in the Americas.

Notes

Notes

CHAPTER 10. MODERN LANGUAGE MOSAICS

CHAPTER INTRODUCTION

Language is an expression of culture, serving to both unite and divide people. The question of which language to use in a multilingual country is an important one since intercultural communication is essential for political stability. Sometimes an existing language will spread worldwide to serve as a means of communication between people, but in regions where several languages and their cultures meet and merge a whole new language may develop. The study of place names, both historical and contemporary, can also reveal much about a culture and its people. In the world of the early twenty-first century, when the cultural composition of many countries is changing, questions about language are of particular significance.

Choosing a Language

The United States has no *official language* (the language selected in multilingual countries to promote internal cohesion and usually the language of the courts and government). The reason for this is simply that if an "official" language were selected for this country it would carry with it the implied preference for the particular culture of which it was the native tongue. It would also imply, rightly or wrongly, that other languages/cultures were not as important.

Historically, languages spread primarily by three means—commerce, religion, and conquest —within the parameters of expansion and/or relocation diffusion. The Indo-European languages spread globally in this manner and one in particular, English, diffused throughout the world during the era of colonialism. Largely because of the political and economic power of Britain and the United States, English today has become the global language of elites, commerce, and business.

Command of English undoubtedly is an advantage throughout the world, and the position of some governments is that the advantages of being able to use English outweigh cultural considerations. Some countries have made English (or another foreign language) their official language, giving indigenous languages secondary status. This provokes charges of neocolonialism or favoring the interest of educated elites. The emotional attachment to language is not just a matter of protecting threatened tongues. It is also a practical issue.

Multilingualism

There is no truly monolingual—where only one language is spoken—country in the world today. Several, such as Japan, Uruguay, Iceland, and Poland, claim monolingualism but even in these countries there are small numbers of people who speak other languages. For example, more than a half-million Koreans live in Japan, and English-speaking Australia has more than 180,000 speakers of aboriginal languages.

Countries in which more than one language is in use are called *multilingual states*. In some of these countries linguistic fragmentation reflects strong cultural pluralism as well as divisive forces (see text Figure 10-5). This is true in former colonial areas where peoples speaking different languages were thrown together, as happened in Africa and Asia. This also occurred in the Americas as text Figure 10-2 shows. Multilingualism takes several forms and can be reflected in regional divisions (Canada, India, Peru, and Belgium), but in some countries (far fewer) there is less regional separation of speakers of different languages (for example, South Africa).

Multilingual countries sometimes solve the problem of intercultural communication by making a foreign tongue their official ("umbrella") language, as shown in Table 10-1. For former colonies, this has often been the language of the colonists, even though they may have gained their independence in a violent revolution against those colonists. Such a policy is not without risks, however, and the long-term results of the use of a foreign language may not always be positive.

Lingua Franca

Traders have often succeeded in overcoming regional linguistic communication problems where language planners failed. Centuries ago people speaking different languages were forced to find ways to communicate for trade. This need resulted in the emergence of a *lingua franca*—any common language spoken by peoples with different native tongues, the result of linguistic convergence. The term comes from the Mediterranean region and its numerous trading posts during the period following the Crusades. In several areas of the world today, linguistic convergence has produced languages of mixed origin. Some of these have developed into major regional languages (see text Figure 10-1).

Toponymy

The study of place names (toponymy) can reveal a great deal about the contents and historical geography of a cultural region. Even when time has erased other evidence, place names can reveal much about a cultural area. Welsh place names in Pennsylvania, French place names in Louisiana, or Dutch place names in Michigan reveal national origin as well as insight into language and dialect, routes of diffusion, and ways of life. Toponyms (place names) make reading a map a fruitful and sometimes revealing experience. A careful eye will spot Roman names on the map of Britain, German names on the map of France, and Dutch names in Australia.

CHAPTER QUIZ

MULTIPLE-CHOICE QUESTIONS

1. The growing Hispanic population has begun to redefine the __?__ states of the United States.
   a. Southern
   b. Northern
   c. Western
   d. Central

2. Which of the following languages has become the one most often used as the primary medium of international communication in business.
   a. French
   b. English
   c. German
   d. Spanish

3. What language was created, and failed, in an effort to allow worldwide communication.
   a. Esperanto
   b. Frankish
   c. Spanenglish
   d. Frenenglish

4. The lingua franca of East Africa is:
   a. Bantu
   b. Swahili
   c. Hausa
   d. Arabic

5. Of the following countries, which has a division between the English and French speakers that may someday lead to a permanent division.
   a. Belgium
   b. France
   c. Canada
   d. Netherlands

6. Which European country has four regions where the people each speak a different language.
   a. Germany
   b. Netherlands
   c. Greece
   d. Switzerland

7. Which West African country has so many languages and lesser tongues that the government adopted English as its "official" language.
   a. Liberia
   b. Mali
   c. Ghana
   d. Nigeria

8. Place names can reveal much about a culture area even after that culture has gone. The study of place names is called:
   a. toponymy
   b. topography
   c. topo-anthropology
   d. topogeogology

9. When African colonies became independent countries, one of the first things they did was:
   a. redraw their boundaries
   b. kick out the government set up by departing colonial masters
   c. change place names
   d. declare an official language

10. In the Stewart system of classification of place names, *Rocky Mountains* is an example of a ___?___ name.
    a. manufactured
    b. possessive
    c. descriptive
    d. commendatory

TRUE/FALSE QUESTIONS

1. In countries where people speak many languages, creating an official language can lead to many problems. (TF)

2. A lingua franca is a combination of French and another language. (TF)

3. During the colonial period, pidgin English developed in the Caribbean region when English was mixed with African languages, and was only spoken by the common people. (TF)

4. Pidgin and creole languages are important unifiers in a linguistically divided region or country. (TF)

5. There are no true monolingual states left in the world today. (TF)

6. In South Africa's past history, language differences led to wars. (TF)

7. It is likely Belgium will follow Czechoslovakia's lead and divide along linguistic lines in the near future. (TF)

8. India has two official languages. (TF)

9. Britain has place names that go back to the time of the Romans. (TF)

10. Place names have different classifications. One is mistake names, caused when people make historical errors in identification or translation. (TF)

STUDY QUESTIONS

1. How did English spread so far? Why are so many countries using it as a second language?

2. Discuss the process of creolization. How is it important in the formation and use of new languages?

3. Study text Figures 10-3, 10-4, 10-5, and 10-6. Relate these figures to information about them in the text. Why do you think some of these countries have had so many problems? Why do you think Switzerland does not have any problem?

4. Why do some countries choose to declare official languages? What are the risks a country faces when it makes such a decision?

5. What does the study of toponymy reveal about past and current cultures of a place? What can we learn from two-part place names?

6. List and define the 10 categories of place names. Try to think of an example of each.

7. List the reasons countries have changed place names.

Notes

Notes

PART FOUR: THE GEOGRAPHY OF RELIGION

CHAPTER 11. RELIGIOUS ORIGINS AND DISTRIBUTIONS

CHAPTER INTRODUCTION

Religion is one of the key components of culture and, like language, can both unify or divide humans. Like language, but in a different way, religion confers identity. Religion dominates the lives and behavior of billions of people worldwide. In the world of the early twenty-first century, modernization, urbanization, secularism, and resurgent fundamentalism appear to be on a collision course. The question facing the world of the twenty-first century will be whether the modern-secular and fundamentalist religious countries can coexist. The study of religion has many geographic dimensions today.

Like languages, religions are constantly changing. In the process, the great religions of the world have diffused across cultural barriers and language boundaries. Persuasion will not lead people to change the language they speak, but it can induce them to convert to a new faith, and conversion still goes on today. Just as the map of languages continues to change, so do patterns of religious affiliation.

The cultural landscape is marked by religion—churches and mosques, cemeteries and shrines, statues and symbols, modes of dress, and personal habits. In industrialized societies, such overt religious displays have declined, but they are still common in more traditional societies.

The Geography of Religion
In many parts of the world, especially in non-Western areas, religion is such a vital part of culture that it practically constitutes the culture. Thus it becomes difficult to define exactly what a religion is, because religion manifests itself in so many different ways. In some societies, religion—at least in organized form—has become less significant in the lives of many people. In many societies in Africa and Asia, religious doctrine exerts tight control over much of the behavior of the people, through ritual and practice and even the orientation of the sleeping body at night. Even where religion is less dominant, its expression is still evident in many practices and beliefs.

Organized religion has powerful effects on human societies. It has been a major force in combating social ills, sustaining the poor, educating the deprived, and advancing medical knowledge. However, religion has also blocked scientific study, supported colonialism and exploitation, and condemned women to an inferior status in many societies. Like other bureaucracies, large-scale organized religion has all too often been unable to adjust to the times.

Major Religions
The distribution of the major religions among various world regions is depicted in text Figure 11-1. The information on this map should be viewed as a generalization of a much more intricate set of distributions. Nevertheless, the map does reveal the dominance of the Christian religions, the several faiths of Christianity having been diffused through European colonialism and aggressive proselytism. Thus Christianity is today the world's most widely dispersed religion (see also Table 11-1). There are more than 1.5 billion Christians in the world today, divided between Roman Catholics (the largest segment), the Protestant churches, and Eastern Orthodox. Together,

61

Christians account for nearly 40 percent of the members of the world's major religions.

The second true *global religion* (also called "universal faiths") is Islam. Despite the fact that it is the "newest" of the global religions, which arose in the western Arabia area in the sixth century, it is today the fastest growing of the world's major religions, and like the others has more than one branch. Islam, like Christianity, has diffused widely, but mainly in Africa and Asia. It dominates in Southwest Asia and North Africa and extends eastward into the former Soviet Union and China, with clusters in Indonesia, Bangladesh, and the Philippines. It even has substantial numbers of adherents in the United States and western Europe. Islam has more than 1 billion adherents, of whom more than half are outside the cultural realm often called the Islamic World. Southwest Asia and North Africa, however, remain the Islamic heartland, with about 400 million adherents.

Christianity and Islam together hold the allegiance of nearly half the world's population (see Table 11-1); no other faith even comes close. Buddhism, another global religion, claims slightly less than 350 million adherents. The third largest faith numerically, Hinduism, is not a global but a cultural faith concentrated in a single geographic realm, and is regarded as the world's oldest organized religion. The vast majority of the 757 million Hindus live in India, although Hinduism extends into Bangladesh, Myanmar, Sri Lanka, and Nepal.

In this chapter we have viewed the spatial distribution of the world's major religions and assessed their strengths in terms of number of adherents. In the next chapter we will examine the three geographic characteristics of religions: their locational origins, routes of diffusion, and their imprints on the cultural landscape.

CHAPTER QUIZ

MULTIPLE-CHOICE QUESTIONS

1. Which South American country, according to text Figure 11-1, has the largest area of Traditional and Shamanist religions.
   a. Argentina
   b. Brazil
   c. Chile
   d. Uruguay

2. Which part of India is not a major area of the Hindu faith.
   a. northeast
   b. south
   c. northwest
   d. southwest

3. The largest division of Christianity in terms of number of adherents is:
   a. Orthodox
   b. Protestant
   c. Sikhism
   d. Roman Catholic

4. The largest number of adherents to the Christian faith are found in:
   a. Europe
   b. Sub-Saharan Africa

c. North America

d. South America

5. The historic roots of Buddhism are found in:
   a. northern India
   b. Sir Lanka
   c. Thailand
   d. China

6. Which of the following is the third largest of the global religions.
   a. Judaism
   b. Hinduism
   c. Islam
   d. Christianity

7. Ethnic religions tend to be spatially concentrated. The principal exception is:
   a. Shintoism
   b. Hinduism
   c. Judaism
   d. Sikhism

8. The rise of secularism can be traced to the rise of:
   a. Roman Catholicism
   b. Greek Orthodoxy
   c. Islam
   d. Protestantism

9. For centuries, Shintoism was the state religion of which of the following countries.
   a. China
   b. Korea
   c. Japan
   d. the Philippines

10. Islam has diffused widely and is considered a world religion, but is mainly found in:
    a. Europe and Asia
    b. Africa and Asia
    c. Africa and Europe
    d. North America and Asia

TRUE/FALSE QUESTIONS

1. In some cultures, religion is a dominating factor. (TF)

2. Religions have never been clearly evident in the cultural landscape. (TF)

3. Religion has condemned women to an inferior status in many societies. (TF)

4. In today's world, Christian religions are the most widely dispersed. (TF)

5. The main division in Islam is between Sunni and Shiite. (TF)

6. The Hindu religion has a bureaucracy similar to that of Christianity and Islam. (TF)

7. Buddhism and Shintoism arose in Japan. (TF)

8. Hinduism is considered a cultural religion in India. (TF)

9. Animistic religions are centered on the belief that animals possess spirits. (TF)

10. Monotheistic religions worship a single deity. (TF)

STUDY QUESTIONS

1. List the different ways religion manifests itself. Although they cannot be defined exactly, list the different rituals that are commonly found in various religions. Also list the positive and negative effects religion has had on people and cultures.

2. Using information from previous chapters, explain how Christianity spread across the globe.

3. Where is the heartland of Islam? Where in this region are the two divisions located?

4. List the ways Hinduism is different from Christianity and Islam.

5. Describe the distribution of Judaism.

6. Where are the source areas for the major religions?

7. List the factors that have led to the rise of secularism. Can you think of other factors in your culture that might play a role (hint: materialism)? List them.

8. What are the true global religions? What are regional religions? Name them and their locations. Where are most traditional religions located?

Notes

Notes

CHAPTER 12.   RELIGIONS: DIFFUSION, AND LANDSCAPE

CHAPTER INTRODUCTION

Religion is the most recent major component of culture to develop. As a result, we know more about the development and dispersal of the major religions than we do of languages. In a world where cultural isolation is a thing of the past and religion is such an important part of culture, it is important to understand the different religions and their effect on the cultures of which they are a part. This chapter traces the spread of the belief systems that have contributed to the formation of modern cultural regions.

It is remarkable that, after tens of thousands of years of human development and migration, the great faiths all arose within a few thousand kilometers of each other in South and Southwest Asia (text Figure 12-1).

Hinduism

Hinduism is the oldest of the world's major religions and one of the oldest extant religions in the world. It is a cultural religion, having emerged without a prophet or a book of scriptures and without evolving a bureaucratic structure comparable to that of the Christian religions. Hinduism appears to have originated in the region of the Indus Valley in what is today Pakistan (see text Figure 12-1), perhaps as much as 4000 years ago. Hinduism reached its fullest development in India, and spread into Southeast Asia before the advent of Christianity. It has not been widely disseminated.

Hinduism has remained essentially a cultural religion of South Asia and is more than a faith; it is a way of life. The cultural landscape of Hinduism is the cultural landscape of India. Temples and shrines, holy animals by the tens of millions, and the sights and sounds of endless processions and rituals all contribute to a unique atmosphere. The faith is a visual as well as an emotional experience.

Buddhism

Buddhism, with fewer than half as many adherents as Hinduism, arose in the sixth century B.C. in India. It was a reaction to the less desirable features of Hinduism such as its strict social hierarchy that protected the privileged and kept millions mired in poverty. Buddhism was founded by Prince Siddhartha, known to his followers as Gautama. The Buddha (enlightened one) was perhaps the first prominent Indian religious leader to speak out against Hinduism's caste system.

The faith grew rather slowly following the Buddha's death until the middle of the third century B.C. when the Emperor Asoka became a convert. During Asoka's rule there may have been more Buddhists than Hindu adherents in India, but after that period the strength of Hinduism began to reassert itself. Today Buddhism is practically extinct in India, although it still thrives in Sri Lanka, Southeast Asia, Nepal, Tibet, Korea, and Japan.

The Buddha received enlightenment as he sat under the Bodhi (enlightenment) tree and because of its association with the Buddha the tree is revered and protected; it has diffused as far as China and Japan and marks the cultural landscape of many villages and towns. Buddhism's architecture includes some magnificent achievements, with the pagoda as perhaps the most familiar structure. Buddhism is experiencing a revival that started two centuries ago and has recently intensified. It has become a global religion and diffused to many areas of the world.

China

Confucianism was founded on the teachings of Confucius in the sixth century B.C. *Taoism* is believed to have been founded by an older contemporary of Confucius, Lao-Tsu, who had great and lasting impacts on Chinese life. In his teachings, Lao-Tsu focused on the proper form of political rule and the oneness of humanity and nature. According to Lao-Tsu, people should learn to live in harmony with nature. Taoism became a cult of the masses.

Following his death, the teachings of Confucius diffused widely throughout East and Southeast Asia. From his writings and sayings emerged the *Confucian Classics*, a set of 13 texts that became the focus of Chinese education for 200 years and the guide for Chinese civilization. In the more liberal atmosphere in communist China today, both the Chinese religions of old *and* the Christian and Islamic faiths are reviving, and Confucianism and Taoism continue to shape Chinese society.

Judaism

Judaism grew out of the belief system of the Jews, one of several nomadic Semitic tribes living in Southwest Asia about 2000 B.C. It is the oldest religion to arise west of the Indus River and the history of the Jews is filled with upheavals. In the face of constant threats, the Jews have sustained their faith, the roots of which lie in the teachings of Abraham, who united his people. Table 11-1 shows the Jewish faith has about 18 million adherents, but the distribution of Jews proves that Judaism is indeed a world religion and has a global importance far greater than its numbers would indicate.

Christianity and Islam

Christianity's three major branches (Roman Catholicism, Protestantism, and Orthodoxy) have diffused throughout the world by expansion combined with relocation diffusion. The cultural landscapes of Christianity's branches reflect the changes the faith has undergone over the centuries. Certain denominations have more durable cultural landscapes in which the authority and influence of the church remain visible.

Islam, the youngest of the world religions, has two major sects, the majority *Sunni* and the minority *Shiah* (see text Figure 12-1). This division occurred almost immediately after the prophet Muhammad's death and took on regional overtones when Shiism became the state religion of Persia (now Iran). Like Christianity, Islam has diffused globally, but is a classic example of expansion diffusion from its Arabian source, followed by relocation diffusion (text Figure 12-4). Islam achieved its greatest artistic expression, its most distinctive visible element, in architecture.

CHAPTER QUIZ

MULTIPLE-CHOICE QUESTIONS

1. Which of the following is the world's oldest major religion.
   a. Judaism
   b. Christianity
   c. Islam
   d. Hinduism

2. Hinduism evolved in what is today the country of:
   a. Pakistan
   b. Nepal
   c. Sri Lanka
   d. India

3. During the sixteenth century, which of the following became a refuge for Hindus with the arrival of Islam and today remains predominately Hindu.
   a. Java
   b. Borneo
   c. Bali
   d. New Guinea

4. Taoism was probably founded by which of the following.
   a. Confucius
   b. Lao-Tsu
   c. Chang-Lee
   d. Mao Tse-tung

5. The oldest global religion to arise west of the Indus River was:
   a. Islam
   b. Christianity
   c. Buddhism
   d. Judaism

6. The continent with the largest population of adherents of the Jewish faith is:
   a. Europe
   b. North America
   c. Asia
   d. South America

7. The worldwide spread of Christianity was accomplished during the era of European colonialism, primarily in which century.
   a. sixteenth
   b. seventeenth
   c. eighteenth
   d. nineteenth

8. The Alhambra Palace was built by members of which of the following religions.
   a. Judaism
   b. Islam
   c. Buddhism
   d. Hindu

9. In the United States, the South's leading religious denomination is:
   a. Lutheran
   b. Catholic

c. Presbyterian

d. Baptist

10. Islam arose in which of the following present-day countries.
    a. Saudi Arabia
    b. Iran
    c. Jordan
    d. Egypt

TRUE/FALSE QUESTIONS

1. The world's great faiths arose in East Asia. (TF)

2. The caste system is part of the Hindu religion. (TF)

3. Hinduism is a very low-key religion, and leaves very little visual evidence on the cultural landscape. (TF)

4. Asoka, emperor of an early Indian state, is credited with the diffusion of Buddhism to distant lands. (TF)

5. Because of the takeover of China by communists, Confucianism no longer has much influence on the people. (TF)

6. Today, Judaism is divided into many branches. (TF)

7. When the Roman Empire became a Christian state and later divided, Emperor Constantine established the Eastern Orthodox Church in Constantinople. (TF)

8. Even today, cathedrals built in Medieval European towns are still a dominating feature on the landscape in some cities. (TF)

9. Christianity marks the cultural landscape with its use of large plots of land for cemeteries. (TF)

10. Islam diffusion is a classic example of expansion diffusion. (TF)

STUDY QUESTIONS

1. Using text Figure 12-1, list the major world religions and their source areas. List their differences and similarities. How have some of these changed over the centuries?

2. Which religions are cultural or regional? Define the difference between cultural and secular. What are some of the traits that make a religion cultural?

3. Which of the major religions was spread by migrant diffusion? What religion replaced it in its source region?

4. Using text Figure 12-4, trace the diffusion of Islam. How does Islam impact its cultural landscape? Discuss Islamic architecture.

Notes

Notes

Notes

CHAPTER 13.   RELIGION, CULTURE, AND CONFLICT

CHAPTER INTRODUCTION

Of the forces shaping the geography of culture, language and religion are two of the most powerful, but as a divisive force religion plays a more prominent role. People may speak the same language but have quite different beliefs either as members of different major religions or different branches of the same faith. As you read this chapter you will gain insight into the perpetuation of cultural strife by religion, a problem that adds to the difficulties of peaceful human coexistence.

It is important for you to realize that religious conflicts usually involve more than differences in spiritual practices and beliefs. Religion functions as a symbol of a much wider set of cultural and political differences. The key points of this chapter are discussed below.

Interfaith Boundaries

Compare text Figure 11-1 with a political map and you will see that some countries lie entirely within the realms of individual world religions, while other countries straddle *interfaith boundaries*, the boundaries between the world's major faiths. Boundaries between major religions that cross countries can be powerful sources of conflict, with serious implications for political cohesion and stability. Examine text Figure 13-1 and you will see that several countries in Africa are in this situation, including Nigeria, Africa's most populous state.

Nigeria is a multilingual country of 110 million inhabitants. Superimposed on its linguistic diversity is religious regionalism: the north is a Muslim zone, whereas Christianity prevails in the south along with local traditional religions. Ethnic groups in the north and south see religion as the focal point of differences, but in reality the potential for a fracturing of the country has numerous causes.

Will Nigeria's location astride an interfaith boundary ultimately destroy the country? The potential for a fracture along religious lines is growing, and any such development would have enormous social and political consequences. Nigeria is a crucible of West African culture and has served as a model for other countries with two or more religious groups within their borders. The breakup of Nigeria would indeed have far-reaching consequences.

Intrafaith Boundaries

Boundaries between branches of a major religion are generally less divisive than boundaries between different religions. A number of Western European countries have Catholic as well as Protestant communities, and often these are reflected in the regional distribution of the population, as in the case of Switzerland (text Figure 13-5). In the early twenty-first century the great majority of these countries were not experiencing religious or ethnic conflict.

But intrafaith boundaries are still capable of producing cultural conflict that can threaten the stability of entire countries. Consider the situation in Northern Ireland, where a Protestant majority and a Catholic minority are in conflict over coexistence and their future. This issue is not strictly religious, but stems from a time when all of Ireland was a British dependency and British Protestants migrated to Ireland. Most settled in the northeastern corner of the island (see text Figure 13-6) where, following partitioning, they constituted the majority of the population and held all the economic and political advantages. The conflict today is over access to opportunities, civil rights, and political influence. But religion and religious history are the banners beneath which the opposing sides march.

Religious Fundamentalism

In the today's world religious leaders and millions of their followers are seeking to return to the basics of their faith. This drive toward *religious fundamentalism* is often born of frustration at the perceived breakdown of society's mores and values, loss of religious authority, failure to achieve economic goals, corruption of political systems, and loss of a sense of local control in the face of the globalization of culture and economy.

People of one society often fear fundamentalism in other societies without recognizing it in their own. In the United States, fundamentalism is often associated with Islam. However, religious fundamentalism is a worldwide phenomenon that affects virtually all religions, including Islam, Christianity, and Hinduism. Fundamentalism and extremism are closely related, and their appeal is global.

Today religions are affected by modernization. Education, radio, television, and travel have diffused notions of individual liberties, sexual equality, and freedom of choice; questions about religions as well as secular authority; and other ideas that may clash with religious dogma.

The drive toward fundamentalism in Christianity and Islam alike is creating a climate of mistrust that could lead to strife. The cultural cores of Christianity and Islam lie in close proximity in Europe and Southwest Asia/North Africa; the prospect of disharmony and conflict between them is growing.

CHAPTER QUIZ

MULTIPLE-CHOICE QUESTIONS

1. When we look at a map of Africa displaying religion locations there is an obvious division where   ?   dominate the north.
    a. Christian religions
    b. Animistic faiths
    c. Muslims
    d. traditional religions

2. In the late 1990s, Ethiopia lost territory with the succession of a predominately Muslim region. That new state is called:
    a. Amharic
    b. Oman
    c. Niger
    d. Eritrea

3. Before the devolution of the former Soviet Union, it was divided into how many Soviet Republics.
    a. 10
    b. 15
    c. 20
    d. 25

4. When the USSR collapsed, the Soviet Republics became independent states. In which of the following is there an interfaith boundary dividing Muslims and Christians that presents a serious problem for the future of the state.
   a. Azerbaijan
   b. Ukraine
   c. Kazakhstan
   d. Belarus

5. In Sri Lanka, the minority Hindu population is in conflict for political recognition by the majority religious group, which is:
   a. Buddhist
   b. Muslim
   c. Christian
   d. Jewish

6. Which Western European country listed below has both Catholic and Protestant adherents living together with little or no religious or ethnic conflict.
   a. Germany
   b. Switzerland
   c. Poland
   d. Ireland

7. The most destructive war of its kind in modern times was a conflict between two Muslim countries following different branches of the Islamic faith. These two countries were:
   a. Syria and Jordan
   b. Iran and Kuwait
   c. Turkey and Greece
   d. Iraq and Iran

8. This North African country suffers from the desire of some groups to create an Islamic Republic.
   a. Tunisia
   b. Morocco
   c. Algeria
   d. Mali

9. In the 1990s, what former European country became a major war zone over interfaith boundaries. This conflict is still going on today.
   a. Bulgaria
   b. Switzerland
   c. Yugoslavia
   d. Turkey

10. In the aftermath of World War I, the creation of Palestine was officially recognized by the:
    a. United Nations
    b. League of Nations

c. World Court

d. Arab League

TRUE/FALSE QUESTIONS

1. Interfaith boundaries keep religious conflicts from occurring. (TF)

2. In Nigeria, religious divisions may end up splitting the country into two republics. (TF)

3. The creation of Pakistan created an almost exclusively Hindu state. (TF)

4. The former Soviet Union created 15 republics and laid them out along religious and linguistic lines. They did such a good job that today, these now independent republics are getting along well. (TF)

5. In Ireland, the majority of the people are protestant. (TF)

6. Fundamentalism and extremism are closely related. (TF)

7. Some Islamic countries are more liberal than others in applying the laws of the Koran. (TF)

8. The interfaith boundaries in former Yugoslavia have finally been resolved and peace restored. (TF)

9. In the 1990s, the Taliban in Afghanistan led the strictest fundamentalist regime in the world. (TF)

10. Recent Muslim attacks in Egypt have hurt the economy. (TF)

STUDY QUESTIONS

1. Going region by region and country by country, as presented in the text, describe the problems of interfaith boundaries. Be sure to study the appropriate maps.

2. Why do many intrafaith boundaries cause less trouble? (Hint: What commonalities do people have)?

3. Where is the most contested religious site in the world located? Why are there so many conflicts over this particular site?

4. Discuss the rise of religious fundamentalism. Is it confined to one religion or many? What are some of the reasons given for this resurgence?

Notes

Notes

PART FIVE: THE POLITICAL IMPRINT

CHAPTER 14. POLITICAL CULTURE AND THE EVOLVING STATE

CHAPTER INTRODUCTION

Political activity is very much a part of human culture and could probably be traced to competition for space or leadership in groups of early humans. Thus emerged history's first politicians. Political activity possesses spatial expression that can be mapped, a fact that interests geographers (*political geography* is the study of political activity in spatial context). The most common line on a map is a political boundary and such boundaries represent a long evolutionary process, but the world political map is relatively new to human history. Perhaps no political map will ever be permanent, as events in the last decade have shown us, but there is hope that political activity may yet lead to a lessening of tensions and conflict between the Earth's inhabitants.

The present-day layout of the world's political map is a product of humanity's endless political-geographic accommodations and adjustments. A mosaic of more than 200 states and territories separated by boundaries make the world looks like a jigsaw puzzle (text Figure 14-1). The map depicting that jigsaw puzzle is the most familiar and widely used map of the world—so widely used that we often fail to think about the pattern it contains. Valuable insights can be obtained from even a brief examination of the nature and significance of the patterns on the political map. It shows, for example, that in terms of territory there are vast inequalities ranging from subcontinental giants to microstates. What the map cannot show is that only a minority of the world states are nation-states, the ideal form to which most nations and states aspire—a political unit wherein the territorial state coincides with the area settled by a certain national group of people. The population of such a country would thus possess a substantial degree of cultural homogeneity and unity—and, hopefully, political stability.

Rise of the Modern State

The concept of statehood spread into Europe from Greece and Rome, where it lay dormant until feudalism began to break down. The Norman invasion of 1066 was perhaps the most significant event in this process. The Normans destroyed the Anglo-Saxon nobility, created a whole new political order, and achieved great national strength under William the Conqueror. On the European mainland, the continuity of dynastic rule and the strength of certain rulers led to greater national cohesiveness. At the same time, Europe experienced something of an economic revival, and internal as well as foreign trade increased. The lifestyles of many disadvantaged people improved and crucial technological innovations occurred. The so-called Dark Ages were over and a new Europe was emerging.

From a political-geographic perspective, the Peace of Westphalia can be seen as the first major step in the emergence of the European state. The treaties signed at the end of the Thirty Years' War (1648) contained language that recognized statehood and nationhood, clearly defined boundaries, and guarantees of security. Europe's political-geographical evolution was to have enormous significance because the European state model was exported through migration and colonialism, but it has not always worked well in the non-Western world.

Territory

No state can exist without territory, although the United Nations does recognize the Palestinians as a stateless nation. Within the state's territory lie the resources that make up the state. The territorial character of states has long interested geographers, who have focused on *territorial morphology*— the territorial size, shape, and relative location. There is no question that the nature of a state's territory can have social and political significance, but focusing on territory alone without considering other aspects of a state's geographical context can be misleading. Being small and compact can mean very different things for a state in the economic core than for one in the periphery.

Different territorial characteristics can present opportunities and challenges, depending on the historical and political-economic context. For the United States, large size, large population, and abundant resources meant emergence as a global power. For the former Soviet Union, the vast distances over which people and resources were distributed presented a serious obstacle and contributed to its collapse. Similar problems can result because of a state's shape—as in the case of the *fragmented* Philippines, the *elongated* Chile, or Thailand with its southern *protruded* area. These and other states' shapes can often cause problems of political control, defense, transportation, or access.

Boundaries

The territories of individual states are separated by international boundaries that mark the limits of national jurisdiction. Boundaries may appear on maps as straight lines or twist and turn to conform to physical or hydrologic features. A *boundary* between states is actually a vertical plane that cuts through the rocks below (called the *subsoil* in legal papers) and the *airspace* above— defined by the atmosphere above a state's land area as marked by its boundaries, as well as what lies at higher altitude (text Figure 14-5). Only where this vertical plane intersects the Earth's surface (on land or at sea) does it form the line we see on a map.

When boundaries were established, things were much different and the resources below the surface were much less well-known than they are today. Many mineral deposits extend from one country to another, provoking arguments about ownership and use. This includes everything from coal deposits and petroleum reserves to groundwater supplies (aquifers). Since aircraft had not yet been invented, little attention was paid to the control of the air above—an issue that is of considerably greater importance today. The control of airline traffic over states' territory may someday be extended to satellite orbits. And air circulates from one airspace to another, carrying pollutants of one state across the vertical plane to another state.

CHAPTER QUIZ

MULTIPLE-CHOICE QUESTIONS

1. A country that is *landlocked* is a country that:
   a. has developed only land transportation
   b. has far more land than people to populate it
   c. has no coast on the open sea
   d. has only one coast on the open sea

2. In the Middle East, the Golan Heights were captured in the 1967 war from:
   a. Syria
   b. Lebanon

c. Jordan
d. Egypt

3. Which of the following is **not** a connotation of the term "nation".
    a. ethnic
    b. linguistic
    c. religious
    d. political

4. The Kurds, a stateless nation, form the largest minority in:
    a. Iraq
    b. Turkey
    c. Iran
    d. Pakistan

5. Just after the beginning of the twentieth century, the world numbered just __?__ Independent countries.
    a. 20
    b. 40
    c. 60
    d. 80

6. Which of the following cannot presently be designated as a nation-state.
    a. Iceland
    b. Poland
    c. Denmark
    d. Russia

7. Which of the following is currently the world's largest state in terms of territory.
    a. India
    b. China
    c. Canada
    d. Russia

8. Which of the following is a good example of an elongated or attenuated state.
    a. Thailand
    b. Chile
    c. France
    d. Mexico

9. The international boundary between the United States and Canada west of the Great Lakes is classified as a __?__ boundary.
    a. superimposed
    b. natural-political
    c. geometric
    d. antecedent

10. Which of the following is **not** an example of a generic political boundary type.
    a. cultural-political
    b. superimposed
    c. antecedent
    d. relic

TRUE/FALSE QUESTIONS

1. The terms country and state are **not** interchangeable. (TF)

2. States tend to jealously guard their territory. (TF)

3. The Kurds are a stateless nation. (TF)

4. Europe in the mid-seventeenth century was a patchwork of ill-defined political entities. (TF)

5. The European nation-state model was adopted around the world. (TF)

6. Elongated and protruded states have basically the same shape. (TF)

7. All landlocked states are surrounded by other states but have access to the sea by rivers. (TF)

8. When state boundaries are established, demarcation is the third stage and all states demarcate their boundaries. (TF)

9. The boundary between former North Vietnam and South Vietnam is a relic boundary. (TF)

10. Boundary disputes generally take five principal forms. (TF)

STUDY QUESTIONS

1. Define state and nation. List the main historic events that led to development of the modern European state and nation-state. Why have most other states followed this model?

2. List the different territorial shapes of states and give examples of each. What problems have been attributed to a state's shape?

3. Why are political boundaries considered to be on a vertical plane? How do boundaries evolve? List the different types of boundaries and what they represent. List and explain the genetic boundary classification pioneered by Hartshorne.

4. What are the functions of boundaries, and how have they changed over time?

5. What are the major reasons for boundary disputes?

Notes

Notes

CHAPTER 15.   STATE ORGANIZATION AND NATIONAL POWER

CHAPTER INTRODUCTION

A state cannot exist without territory and this component can be expressed spatially on a map (text Figure 14-1) in several ways. Careful study of such a map tells us much about world political units even at the scale of a world map, and raises intriguing questions. Organizational ability and preference are intrinsic cultural attributes of humans and the political map of the world states expresses this quite clearly. The forces at work in the shaping of a state provoke both unity and division and some states may fracture, but cooperation and tolerance can produce success under almost any circumstances. That fact offers the best hope for solving the problems of humanity in the early twenty-first century.

Most political geographers believe that in the near future the total number of independent states will surpass the nearly 200 existing today. These 200 countries will occupy the surface of a small planet of which over two-thirds is covered by water or ice. With such a large number of entities, some large and others very small, some well-endowed and some poor, it is inevitable that equality will remain a mirage. We now turn to a consideration of the human and organizational dimensions of the state.

Large-Scale Influences on State Power

Patterns of economic and political power are one of the most important long-term influences on the situation of a country and the measure of the relative power of a state. If you want to understand the present map of world states (text Figure 14-1) then you need only compare it to text Figure 15-1, which shows the influence of four centuries (1550–1950) of dominant colonial influences. The modern world political map owes its genesis to this pattern.

The pattern and influences of the colonial era laid the foundation, more than 400 years ago, for a global capitalist economy by knitting together the economics of widely separated areas. One view today—World-Systems Analysis—portrays the world as divided into three tiers referred to as core, periphery, and semi-periphery. While there is considerable debate about the categories associated with this view and the heavy emphasis on economic factors, it nonetheless encourages the view of the world political map as a system of interlinking parts and the necessity to understand their relationships.

Cores and Capitals

A well-developed primary core area and a mature capital city are essential components of a well-integrated state. *Core* refers to the center, heart, or focus. The core of a nation-state is constituted by the national heartland—the largest population cluster, the most productive region, the area with the greatest centrality and accessibility, probably containing the capital city as well. Countries without recognizable cores (Chad, Mongolia, Bangladesh) may have notable capitals, but these alone do not produce a well-integrated state. Some states possess more than one core area, and such *multicore states* confront particular problems. If the primary core is dominant, as in the United States, such problems may be slight. In a country like Nigeria, where three core areas (none truly dominant) mark ethnically and culturally diverse parts of the state (text Figure 15-5), serious problems arise.

The core area is the heart of the state; the *capital city* is the brain. This is the political nerve center of the country, its national headquarters and seat of government, and the center of national life. This special status is often recognized by using the name of a country's capital interchangeably with that of the state itself. The primacy of the capital is yet another manifestation of the European state model, one that has diffused worldwide. In general, the capital city is the pride of the state, and its layout, prominent architectural landmarks, public art, and often its religious structures reflect the society's values and priorities. It is the focus of the state as a political region.

Unitary and Federal Systems

All states confront divisive forces—some strong enough to threaten their very survival. The question is how best to adjust the workings of the state to ensure its continuity. When the nation-state evolved in Europe, this was not a problem. Democracy as we know it today had not yet matured; governments controlled the use of force and could suppress dissent by forceful means. There seemed to be no need to accommodate minorities or outlying regions where the sense of national identity was weaker. The European state model was a *unitary state* and its administrative framework was designed to ensure the central government's authority over all parts of the state.

European notions of the state diffused to much of the rest of the world, but in the New World and former colonies elsewhere these notions did not always work well. When colonies freed themselves of European dominance, many found that conditions in their newly independent countries did not lend themselves to unitary government, and such situations led to the emergence of the *federal state*. Federalism accommodated regional interests by vesting primary power in provinces, states, or other regional units over all matters except those explicitly given to the national governments. The Australian geographer K.W. Robinson described federation as "the most geographically expressive of all political systems... federation enables unity and diversity to coexist." Canada, Australia, Brazil, Nigeria, and India are examples of federal governments existing today.

Opposing Forces

All states suffer in some measure from disruptive forces, and all states possess unifying bonds. Strengthening these bonds to overcome divisions is a principal task of government. States are held together by *centripetal forces* such as nationalism, education, circulation (the system of integration of and movement through language, education, transportation, and transportation), and the institutions of government. By manipulating the system, many countries have managed to enhance the centripetal forces that shape unity.

States must also deal with divisive or *centrifugal forces* in the form of ethnic disunity, cultural differences, or regional disparities. When these centrifugal forces outweigh the centripetal ones described above, the state will collapse. In recent times we have witnessed the disintegration of the world's largest colonial empires, including, in the mid 1990s, the Soviet Union. Yugoslavia collapsed when a quasi-federal system failed to withstand the forces of division. In the early twenty-first century, centrifugal forces seem to be on the rampage.

Power Relationships

Just as some states are large and others are small, some are rich and others poor, so there are powerful states and weak ones. Measuring the power of states is a complex and imprecise business. There can be no doubt, however, that a state's power is directly related to its capacity for organization. *Geopolitics*, a century-old part of political geography, studies the power relationships among states. Current developments in the states of the Pacific Rim fuel an old debate on Eurasian power relationships.

CHAPTER QUIZ

MULTIPLE-CHOICE QUESTIONS

1. At the beginning of the twenty-first century the third largest global economy belonged to:
   a. India
   b. Japan
   c. Germany
   d. China

2. The height of the colonial era came during the __?__ centuries.
   a. nineteenth and twentieth
   b. eighteenth and nineteenth
   c. fifteenth and sixteenth
   d. seventeenth and eighteenth

3. The state of Nigeria has __?__ core areas.
   a. four
   b. two
   c. three
   d. five

4. In the late 1990s, which of the following countries was building a new, ultramodern capital city to symbolize its rapid economic growth and modernization.
   a. Brazil
   b. Malaysia
   c. the Philippines
   d. China

5. The geographic term *rimland* was coined by:
   a. Halford Mackinder
   b. Karl Hausofer
   c. Carl Saur
   d. Nicholas Spykman

6. A global capitalist economy began to develop around:
   a. 1850
   b. 1650
   c. 1450
   d. 1950

7. Outside the European realm two countries built colonial empires. These were:
   a. India and Pakistan
   b. Japan and Russia
   c. China and Japan
   d. Russia and China

8. The continent that had the greatest number of different colonial powers represented was:
   a. South America
   b. Africa
   c. Asia
   d. North America

9. The originator of the *heartland theory* was:
   a. Karl Haushofer
   b. Friedrich Ratzel
   c. Nicholas Spykman
   d. Halford Mackinder

10. In the United States, the capital city was built on federal territory originally taken from which two states.
    a. Maryland and Virginia
    b. Virginia and North Carolina
    c. Maryland and Delaware
    d. Delaware and Virginia

TRUE/FALSE QUESTIONS

1. The ideal population for a state is the internal carrying capacity. (TF)

2. The term *forward capital* refers to a capital city that is moving ahead economically. (TF)

3. A federal state creates unity by accommodating regional differences. (TF)

4. Nigeria's northern core area represents the Christian heart of the country. (TF)

5. Alaska was originally part of Russia's colonial empire. (TF)

6. Heartland theory proposed that land-based power, not ocean dominance, would rule the world. (TF)

7. At the end of World War II, the world was bipolar. (TF)

8. The primacy of the capital city of a state is a manifestation of the European model, but it did **not** diffuse globally. (TF)

9. There are signs a multipolar world is again forming. (TF)

10. Some governments create artificial crises to bring the people together and lessen internal conflict. (TF)

STUDY QUESTIONS

1. Explain why economic success and political power are closely linked. What role did colonialization play in the establishment of today's states?

2. How do core areas influence a state's success? What are the functions of capital cities within a core area and those outside the core area?

3. What is the difference between unitary and federal systems? List the unifying and divisive forces of each. What role does nationalism play in unifying a state, and how do governments manipulate this feeling? Why is the Nigerian government having problems keeping the country unified?

4. List the events that led the world to become multipolar during the nineteenth and early twentieth centuries. How did World War II change this? List the main reasons we will be living in a multipolar world again.

Notes

Notes

Notes

CHAPTER 16.   MULTINATIONALISM ON THE MAP

<u>CHAPTER INTRODUCTION</u>

The world today presents a complex map of political entities outlined by lines representing political boundaries. Such lines show the geographic limits of the political unit, but actually represent much more. Originally serving primarily as trespass lines to indicate the limits of claim to a portion of the Earth by a group or culture, time and technology have combined to demand that they be quite precise, a condition fairly new in human history. Most boundaries were established before much was known about the interior of the earth and the resources that lay hidden there. Add to this the increasing activity of many states in controlling adjacent areas and you begin to appreciate the enormity of the problems. Like other components of human culture, boundaries represent a history of adjustment, evolution, and experience That must adjust to new conditions and circumstances if they are to be beneficial to humanity.

Ours is a world of contradictions. At every turn we are reminded of the interconnections of nations, states, and regions, yet separatism and calls for autonomy are rampant. In the early twenty-first century, we appear to be caught between the forces of division and unification. Despite these conflicts and contradictions there is today hardly a country in existence that is not involved in some multinational association. There is ample proof that such association is advantageous to the partners and that being left out can have serious negative effects on state and nation.

Supranationalism
The phenomenon of interstate cooperation is quite old. In ancient Greece, city-states formed leagues to protect and promote mutual benefits. This practice was imitated many centuries later by the cities of Europe's Hanseatic League. But the degree to which this idea has taken root in the modern world is unprecedented. The twentieth century witnessed the establishment of numerous international associations in political, economic, cultural, and military spheres, giving rise to the term *supranationalism* (technically, the efforts by three or more states to forge associations for mutual benefit and in pursuit of shared goals).

Supranational unions range from global organizations such as the United Nations and its predecessor, the League of Nations, to regional associations such as the European Union. All formed in the twentieth century they signified the inadequacy of the state system as a framework for dealing with important issues and problems. Today, in the early twenty-first century, there are more than 100 supranational organizations, counting subsidiaries. The more states participate in such multilateral associations, the less likely they are to act alone in pursuit of a self-interest that might put them at odds with neighbors.

League of Nations to United Nations
The modern beginnings of the supranational movement came with the conferences that followed the end of World War I. The concept of an international organization that would include all the states of the world led to the creation of the League of Nations in 1919. The league was born of a world-wide desire to prevent future aggression, but the failure of the United States to join dealt the organization a severe blow. It collapsed in the chaos of the beginning of World War II, but it had spawned other organizations such as the Permanent Court of International Justice, which would become the International Court of Justice after World War II. It also initiated the first international negotiations on maritime boundaries and related aspects of the law of the sea.

The United Nations was formed at the end of World War II to foster international security and cooperation. Representation of countries in the United Nations has been more universal than it was in the League (text Figure 16-1). In 1998, there were 185 member states with only a handful of states still not members. It is important to remember that the United Nations is not a world government; member states participate voluntarily but may agree to abide by specific UN decisions.

Among the functions of the United Nations the imposition of international sanctions and mobilization of peacekeeping operations are the most high-profile. Peacekeeping has become a costly and controversial responsibility in the middle of 2001, more than 40,000 peacekeeping troops were serving in various countries around the world. The organization's peacekeeping function provides major benefits to the international community. Another arena in which the United Nations has accomplished much is the *law of the sea,* through which are channeled the extensions of national claims over the oceans (see text Figure 16-2).

Regional Multinational Unions

The global manifestation of international cooperation is most strongly expressed at the regional level. States have begun to join together to further their political ideologies, economic objectives, and strategic goals. Among many regional multinational associations, the European Union is the most complex and far reaching. Originally known as *Benelux,* it was formed by Belgium, the Netherlands, and Luxembourg before the end of World War II. Today, the 15 member states (text Figure 16-4) are likely to be joined by others within a decade.

Economic, military, cultural, and political forces are today affecting the activities of more than 60 major international organizations. The main motives for supranational cooperation are economic, but they are not the only ones. Along with economic prosperity, a shared military threat (as concerns the North Atlantic Treaty Organization [NATO] for example), appears to be equally strong in promoting international cooperation.

CHAPTER QUIZ

MULTIPLE-CHOICE QUESTIONS

1. The beginnings of the supranational movement came with the conferences that followed the end of:
   a. WW I
   b. WW II
   c. the Korean War
   d. the Gulf War

2. Which of the following functions of the United Nations has become the most costly and controversial.
   a. maintaining its own armed force
   b. boundary demarcation
   c. peacekeeping
   d. refugee control

3. By 1998, how many members were there in the Unrepresented Nations and Peoples Organization (UNPO).
    a. 65
    b. 49
    c. 15
    d. 39

4. Which of the following countries was the first to announce that it claimed not only the continental shelf adjacent to its coast but also the waters lying above it.
    a. Chile
    b. Peru
    c. the United States
    d. Argentina

5. The Territorial Sea designation allows countries to claim state sovereignty for a distance of _?_ nautical miles from their shorelines.
    a. 12
    b. 18
    c. 24
    d. 30

6. In 1998, there were more than _?_ multinational unions in the world.
    a. 40
    b. 50
    c. 60
    d. 70

7. The original name of the group that would ultimately become the European Union was:
    a. the Common Market
    b. Benelux
    c. the European Community
    d. the European Free Trade Union

8. Which member of the European Union is a concern for other members because of a possible dominance of the organization.
    a. England
    b. France
    c. Sweden
    d. Germany

9. Which member of the European Union joined as a result of legislative action rather than a referendum of the people of the country.
    a. England
    b. Denmark
    c. France
    d. Germany

10. Progress toward European unification depends on:
    a. military alliances
    b. agreements on refugee questions
    c. economics
    d. common currency decision

TRUE/FALSE QUESTIONS

1. Supranationalism is a twentieth century phenomenon. (TF)

2. International sanctions are designed to praise a country for its good behavior. (TF)

3. The WHO is a part of the United Nations. (TF)

4. The Truman Proclamation territorially claimed the continental shelves of the United States, and the sea above them. (TF)

5. Benelux was the first interstate economic union. (TF)

6. Today, interstate cooperation is widespread all around the world. (TF)

7. Germany dominates the current EU. (TF)

8. Any European country can join the EU. (TF)

9. Political motives lie behind the forming of most all interstate unions. (TF)

10. NATO is a military alliance between states, and membership is now spreading eastward in Europe. (TF)

STUDY QUESTIONS

1. Define supranationalism. Why is it important?

2. Why did the League of Nations fail? Did it accomplish anything?

3. What was the primary reason for the formation of the United Nations? List and describe its subsidiaries and their purposes.

4. List the main points in the process that led to ratification of the law of the sea, and include the history. How does this law affect an ocean-fronting country's boundaries?

5. Discuss the history leading to the formation of the EU. What problems does this organization face? In what other parts of the world are international associations being formed to reduce economic barriers?

Notes

Notes

CHAPTER 17.   THE CHANGING GLOBAL POLITICAL LANDSCAPE

CHAPTER INTRODUCTION

The world today is a world of contradictions. Hopes for peace and cooperation are often countered by the reality of division resulting from national self-interest, economic factors, human rights issues, and many other concerns. The hopes for a so-called New World Order shaped by forces that interconnect nations and states by supranational blocks capable of balancing the forces of the major powers, and multinational action should any state violate rules of communal conduct, are already clouded by doubts and uncertainties. The world today is burdened by a weakening state system and devolution, which afflicts a growing number of countries.

The focus in this chapter is on the forces that are changing the global political landscape. These are forces with which governments, businesses, and individuals must contend. To be aware of these forces is to be better prepared to cope with them. When we study the changes taking place in the world's political framework, we enter the field of *geopolitics*. This field combines geography with some aspects of political science, but geography brings cultural, environmental, and spatial perspectives to the field. As such, geopolitics is a wide arena that helps us understand the forces that are transforming the world map.

Forces of Devolution

Devolution, the disintegration of a state along regional lines, is occurring in a growing number of countries, old and young, large and small, wealthy and poor. States are the result of political-geographical evolution that may have spanned millennia (China) or centuries (many European states). Still others have evolved from colonial empires only a few decades ago, as in much of Africa. Revolution, civil war, and international conflict accompany the evolution of states. Even the oldest and apparently most stable states are vulnerable to a process that is the reverse of evolution, propelled by forces that divide and destabilize. That process is called *devolution*.

Devolution results from many factors, and rarely is the process propelled by a single one, but the primary ones are *cultural*, *economic*, and *spatial*. In Europe, devolutionary forces threaten a large number of older as well as younger states (text Figure 17-1). Several of these have cultural bases, as in Spain, Belgium, and the former Yugoslavia. Economic *and* cultural devolutionary forces are present in Catalonia, but purely economic forces are at work in Italy and France (which is often cited as the model nation-state). In this case the problem is the island of Corsica, where the activists want power and money. Europe is not alone in confronting economic forces leading to devolution. During the 1990s a devolutionary movement arose in Brazil that was rooted in economics. It seems that no country is immune from devolutionary pressures.

If devolutionary events have one feature in common, it is that they occur on the margins of states. Note that every one of the devolutionary infected areas shown in text Figure 17-1 lies on a coast or a boundary. Distance, remoteness, and peripheral location are allies of devolution. In many cases the regions adjoin neighbors that may support separatist objectives. As stated previously, the basic reason for almost all devolutionary forces is territory under one guise or another.

In most instances of devolution, the problem remains domestic; that is, it has little or no impact on the world at large. One notable exception is the devolution of the former Soviet Union by a powerful combination of political, cultural, and economic forces (text Figure 17-3). When this occurred, the world was transformed. The former Soviet empire is left with a political-geographic legacy that will remain problematic for generations to come. Visions of local or regional autonomy, notions of democracy and participation, concepts of religious fundamentalism, and economic globalization are changing the map of the modern world.

The State in the New World Order

The state is the crucial building block in the global international framework, yet the world today is burdened by a weakening state system and an antiquated boundary framework. The state's weaknesses are underscored by the growing power of regions, provinces, States, and other internal entities to act independently of the national government. The European state system, born more than 350 years ago, was exported globally with government. Europeanization in autocratic form, later modified in many instances to a federal system, was at best tenuous in non-European areas. Many boundaries in existence today are the result of colonial control and decision with little regard for the impact on indigenous populations. With the end of colonialism, the legacy of such decisions has produced devolution and conflict. Supranationalism may be a solution to at least some of these problems, but the state system did not evolve quickly or painlessly and it is doubtful its successor, whatever that may be, will proceed more smoothly.

A New World Order is said to be in the making following the end of the Cold War, but its geographic outlines cannot yet be discerned. It is likely to involve a multipolar rather than a bipolar configuration (as existed before the devolution of the former Soviet Union), and it is unclear how orderly it will be or who the key players will be.

CHAPTER QUIZ

MULTIPLE-CHOICE QUESTIONS

1. The common currency of the European Union is the:
    a. lira
    b. euro
    c. dollar
    d. mark

2. In 1997, which of the following European countries was **not** facing serious devolutionary pressures.
    a. Scotland
    b. Belgium
    c. Italy
    d. Germany

3. The province of Catalonia is a part of which country.
    a. Spain
    b. France
    c. Italy
    d. Portugal

4. In the past decade, which two East European countries have succumbed to devolutionary pressures.
    a. Bulgaria and Yugoslavia
    b. Poland and Hungary
    c. Czechoslovakia and Yugoslavia
    d. Poland and Czechoslovakia

5. In this South Asian country the Sinhalese majority has been unable to suppress the demands of the Tamil minority for an independent state.
    a. India
    b. Sri Lanka
    c. Indonesia
    d. Bangladesh

6. In the United States the first real brush with devolution may come in which state.
    a. Alaska
    b. Florida
    c. Washington
    d. Hawai'i

7. Before the Soviet Union devolved, it was composed of how many Soviet republics.
    a. 10
    b. 15
    c. 20
    d. 25

8. We are entering the twenty-first century with a boundary system rooted in the __? century.
    a. seventeenth
    b. eighteenth
    c. twentieth
    d. nineteenth

9. Which of the following is **not** one of the likely candidates to be included as dominating state in a New World order.
    a. Canada
    b. China
    c. India
    d. Europe

10. Following the collapse of the former Soviet Union, Moscow's most serious devolutionary problem was centered in:
    a. Chechnya
    b. Turkestan
    c. Belarus
    d. Georgia

TRUE/FALSE QUESTIONS

1. State devolution is the reverse of state evolution. (TF)

2. In Italy devolution is caused by economic problems between the north and south. (TF)

3. Devolutionary processes tend to occur in the middle of states. (TF)

4. The removal of the Berlin Wall was a result of the devolution of the former Soviet Union. (TF)

5. Most of the 15 newly independent former Soviet republics suffer from centrifugal forces. (TF)

6. The new Russia is a unitary state. (TF)

7. The great majority of supranational alliances bind together states that lie among geographic realms. (TF)

8. In some countries, religious fundamentalism appeals to people where prospects for democracy are dim or oppression seems inescapable. (TF)

9. The ability of small countries to acquire nuclear weapons poses a serious danger to the whole world. (TF)

10. A New World Order will probably be established very early in the twenty-first century. (TF)

STUDY QUESTIONS

1. Explain the devolutionary process. Does culture always play a role in this process? How have devolutionary factors affected particular European countries? Name the countries and list the factors involved.

2. List the factors involved in the break-up of Yugoslavia. Why was this such a tragic and complicated situation? Has it been resolved?

3. Spatially, where does devolution usually occur? Why? Where does the United States have devolutionary forces at work today?

4. Explain the devolution of the former Soviet Union. What devolutionary factors are now being faced in the newly independent republics?

5. How is the position of the state changing in today's world? Are we heading for a New World Order? What are the options this new world order might take?

Notes

Notes

PART SIX: LIFE IN THE RURAL SECTOR

CHAPTER 18.   TRADITIONAL LIVELIHOODS OF RURAL PEOPLES

CHAPTER INTRODUCTION

All humans engage in some form of activity to provide food, clothing, shelter, and the other amenities of life, but the varied activities of today owe their success to decisions of the past. The development of agriculture may well be the single most important development in human history. Its success supported both rural and urban populations. With the combination of agriculture and technology lies the ability to provide food and security for all humanity. How, and if, this challenge is met will determine the future of our species.

Economic Activity
Economic activities range from simple to complex, from ancient to modern. One way to classify these activities is to distinguish among different *types* of activities. For many years three basic types of economic activities were recognized: primary, the *extractive sector*, secondary, the *production sector*, and tertiary, the *service sector*. Rural life has long been dominated by primary economic activities, hunting and gathering (ancient means of survival), farming of all kinds, livestock herding, fishing, forestry, and lumbering. Here workers and the natural environment come into direct contact and the environment sometimes suffers.

Agriculture
The deliberate tending of crops and livestock in order to produce food and fiber is properly called *agriculture*, an activity that may be less than 12,000 years old and emerged sequentially in several regions of the world. When humans embraced agriculture they changed the world and human culture forever. Food supplies became more dependable and quantities increased. This in turn led to population increases and, eventually, permanent settlements. Agriculture changes more of the Earth's surface than any other human activity and thus creates a *cultural landscape* that is reflective of the numbers, cultivation practices, settlement patterns, and other cultural characteristics of the population. It is the reason why huge numbers of humans can successfully occupy Earth today.

Revolutions
Agriculture actually developed in several stages, referred to as *revolutions* because of the changes in the way it was practiced. The First Agricultural Revolution achieved plant domestication, a gradual process that was global, often including duplicate domestication of certain plants in differ-ent parts of the world, and extending over a period of several thousand years. Humans learned about such things as plant selection, primitive methods of cultivation, and irrigation. Early agriculture was undoubtedly combined with gathering and some hunting as well as animal domestication.

The Second Agricultural Revolution, beginning in the latter part of the so-called Middle Ages, involved improved methods of cultivation, production, and storage. Exact points of origin are unknown but it seems certain that the process was gradual and centered in Europe. The hall-mark of this revolution was improved production and organization. Without these changes, the

Industrial Revolution would not have been possible and it in turn sustained the changes that were taking place in agriculture.

The Third Agriculture Revolution is based on research and technology in plant genetics. It occurred at a time when the population explosion seemed to threaten the global food supply in the manner that Thomas Malthus had predicted two centuries earlier. The laboratory-developed new, higher-yielding strains of grains and other crops seemed to suggest that the threat of global famine was a thing of the past. However, the race between population growth and food production is not over, and it remains to be seen whether the Third Agricultural Revolution can continue to over-come the challenge.

Survival

Subsistence agriculture, which produces little or no surplus and involves hundreds of millions of people in a struggle for survival, still prevails in large regions of tropical Africa, Asia, and the Americas. Here farmers grow food only to survive. Very likely they do not even own the soil that they till. Some subsistence farmers may, in fact, practice *shifting cultivation*, a method of tillage where plots are farmed until the soil is depleted and then the farmers move on and clear a new field. As many as 200 million people still subsist in this manner in tropical regions of Africa, Middle America, and South America, using methods that have not changed in thousands of years.

Sedentary or shifting, subsistence farming is not only a way of life but a state of mind for those who practice it. Experience has taught these farmers and their families that times of comparative plenty will be followed by times of scarcity. It should also serve to remind us that the security of plentiful food supplies in the technically advanced, wealthier countries is not shared by much of the Earth's population.

CHAPTER QUIZ

MULTIPLE CHOICE QUESTIONS

1. In which of the following economic sectors do we find the activity of farming:
   a. production
   b. marketing
   c. extractive
   d. service

2. Farming started about __?__ years ago.
   a. 8,000
   b. 10,000
   c. 12,000
   d. 14,000

3. The first tools used by humans in hunting were:
   a. made of stone
   b. simple clubs
   c. beaten into shape using copper
   d. more complex than we first realized

4. Fishing probably started:
   a. before hunting
   b. 200,000 years ago
   c. during the last ice age when men could fish through the ice
   d. when the water warmed and covered the continental shelves at the end of the last ice age

5. The first agricultural methods probably involved the:
   a. the sowing of seeds
   b. planting of roots and cuttings
   c. transplanting whole plants
   d. importing of food plants from other regions

6. Wild cattle may have first been domesticated for:
   a. use as draft animals
   b. their milk
   c. religious purposes
   d. their hides to build shelters

7. The earliest animals to be domesticated in Africa were:
   a. guinea fowl
   b. cattle
   c. chickens
   d. goats

8. Which of the following plays a big part in shifting cultivation.
   a. nomadic existence
   b. very fertile soil
   c. high population density
   d. control of fire

9. The colonial powers introduced forced farming in their colonies to:
   a. improve the lifestyle and wealth of the farmers
   b. make profits for themselves
   c. help farmers diversify their crops
   d. help farmers hold their communities together

10. Which of the following statements is **not** true about the Second Agricultural Revolution.
    a. it allowed people to live in larger urban clusters
    b. it started quickly and spread rapidly
    c. tools and equipment were modified and improved
    d. more efficient food storage and distribution was created

TRUE/FALSE QUESTIONS

1. The United States has more farmers than most countries. (TF)

2. Worldwide, people tend to eat more meat than vegetable products. (TF)

3. Drought is the worst enemy of present-day hunting and gathering societies. (TF)

4. Agriculture transforms whole countrysides. (TF)

5. The development of stone tools never became very important in helping early humankind progress. (TF)

6. By using just fishing, hunting, and some gathering, various groups were able to establish some permanence in settlement. (TF)

7. Agriculture first started in the Americas. (TF)

8. It is now believed the Chinese may have been among the world's first farmers. (TF)

9. It is not possible to identify in which region any animal was first domesticated. (TF)

10. In the strictest use of the word, subsistence farming means farmers who only grow enough food to supply themselves and their family. (TF)

STUDY QUESTIONS

1. Discuss how hunting and gathering societies existed before agriculture. How did they live? What kind of tools did they devise and use? Why was the use of fire so important?

2. How did fishing change the lives of our early ancestors? Was their life any better? What means did they use to catch fish?

3. Using text Figure 18-2 and Table 18-1, identify the sources of the many domesticated plants. Does the source of food plants you recognize surprise you? How many can you recognize as being something you have seen in your local grocery store?

4. Read the section on animal domestication and diffusion. Why was this such an important development in human history? Why do you think chickens are kept by so many societies worldwide? Why do you think Africa is trying to domesticate more animals today?

5. Discuss the ways colonial powers permanently changed farming practices when they colonized the different areas of the world.

Notes

Notes

CHAPTER 19.   LANDSCAPES OF RURAL SETTLEMENT

CHAPTER INTRODUCTION

The basic human needs are food, clothing, and shelter. Of these, buildings reveal the most about a culture and those who build them, as a visible expression of the culture. When large permanent settlements evolved, buildings became more substantial, specialized, and permanent. As culture became more complex the simple practicality of adaptation to, and protection from, the elements was expanded to include functional differentiation, reflecting the changing needs of people and culture.

Where People Live

Early humans all lived in "rural" areas. They were few in numbers and generally mobile. It was not until the development of agriculture that "permanent" settlements became the norm. As recently as several hundred years ago the vast majority of humans still resided in rural areas, generally in agricultural villages, raising crops or livestock to support themselves. Towns and cities were few and the exception rather than the norm. It was a very different world than residents of modern, technically advanced cultures experience today.

In today's world, about half the population still resides in rural areas. This is because the vast majority of humanity still farms the land, often in ways that have not changed significantly. In portions of East and South Asia as many as three out of four residents may live in a rural area. By contrast, in the United States, Canada, Western European countries, Japan, and Australia there are far more urban than rural dwellers, reflecting changes in industrialization, transportation, and urbanization over the last 100 years.

Rural Dwellings

The *cultural landscape* is the human imprint on the Earth's surface, and no human activity produces a more visible cultural landscape than agriculture. Much can be learned about a culture by observing rural settlement patterns. The forms, functions, building materials, and the spacing of rural dwellings reveal much about a region and its culture. The compact, crowded agricultural villages of India, for example, designed to conserve land for actual farming, stand in sharp contrast to the widely scattered individual farmsteads of the American Great Plains where more land may be occupied by buildings on each farm than the Indian farmer has for cultivation.

Social and economic opportunities and needs, natural environments, and traditions are also cultural characteristics that are revealed in the rural settlement scene. Large, elaborate dwellings reflect prosperity or social standing while a church, temple, or other place of worship reveals something about the priorities of the culture. Dwellings may be concentrated along and near a road or waterway, suggesting available transportation, on high ground, suggesting concern about frequent flooding, or on, say, southern slopes reflecting, concerns about the winter months (this could also indicate a location in the Northern Hemisphere).

Building Materials

Except in the wealthier societies, most humans construct their dwellings of whatever local material is available commensurate with their experience and the natural environment. Wattle, wood, brick, and stone are among the building materials used in domestic architecture. The selection of the building material is also an indication of the climate of the region. Traditional rural societies are not wealthy and therefore cannot afford, for example, to import wood from great distances if it is not immediately available locally. Log houses require considerable labor, to say nothing of available timber and transportation needs. They usually indicate a period of severe winter. Cut wood (lumber) is not immediately available in many areas and is expensive. The appearance of elaborate wood or brick dwellings in a region such as the North American Great Plains indicates wealth and an elaborate transportation system. Stone is a common building material if available locally and has great durability. Like wood, its appearance in the dwellings of a region considerably removed from local supplies indicates something about the affluence and social standing of the culture and its inhabitants.

Settlement Patterns
The form or layout of rural villages reflects historical circumstances, the nature of the land, and economic conditions. They range from linear and clustered to circular and grid pattern. Each has something to say about the culture that built them.

Early villages had to be near a reliable water supply, be defensible, and have sufficient land nearby for cultivation to name but a few concerns. They also had to adapt to local physical and environmental conditions, conditions which can be identified with a practiced eye. In Nepal in the Himalayan Mountains, villages cling to the slopes above the river bottoms, indicating awareness of spring floods with the melting of winter snows. Villages in the Netherlands are linear, crowded on the dikes surrounding land reclaimed from the sea. Grid-patterned villages in much of Latin America reflect the influence of their Spanish founders while circular villages in parts of Africa indicate a need for a safe haven for livestock at night. A careful examination of the rural settlement of a region reveals much about the culture, its history, and its traditions.

CHAPTER QUIZ

MULTIPLE-CHOICE QUESTIONS

1. In hamlets or villages where houses and other buildings are grouped in clusters, they are said to have a:
   a. nucleated settlement pattern
   b. dispersed settlement pattern
   c. linear settlement pattern
   d. elongated settlement pattern

2. Which of the following probably did **not** affect how our ancestors of 100,000 years ago built their shelters.
   a. flood-prone areas
   b. hot weather
   c. ideas from neighboring villages
   d. available building materials

3. In which direction did the New England house style diffuse the farthest.
   a. north
   b. south
   c. southwest
   d. west

4. Which of the following was **not** a characteristic of the early Southern style house in the United States.
    a. a characteristic porch
    b. often built on a raised platform
    c. often built on a stone foundation
    d. usually had two stories

5. In China today, why are the farm and village houses being built of baked-mud walls and thatch roofs, when in past times they were made of brick and had tile roofs.
    a. scarcity of building materials
    b. people don't plan on living in the same place so long
    c. styles have changed
    d. it is cheaper and quicker

6. The modern house type is most common in:
    a. Western Europe
    b. Japan
    c. the United States
    d. Canada

7. The log house probably originated in:
    a. East Asia
    b. northern Europe
    c. central Africa
    d. Mexico

8. Wood is generally the preferred building material for houses. If it is not available, the next most likely material is:
    a. wattle
    b. stone
    c. brick
    d. grass and brush

9. The cadastral system to delineate property lines adopted by the U.S. government after the American Revolution was specifically designed to:
    a. produce a pleasing cultural landscape
    b. facilitate ease of legal registration of ownership
    c. facilitate even dispersal of settlers across farmlands of the interior
    d. facilitate ease of legal description

10. The smallest cluster of houses and nonresidential buildings is known as a:
    a. village
    b. hamlet
    c. town
    d. rundling

TRUE/FALSE QUESTIONS

1. In the United States Midwest, rural houses tend to be laid out in a nucleated settlement pattern. (TF)

2. Our distant ancestors made their first homes in caves. (TF)

3. Communal living developed as human society developed and became more specialized. (TF)

4. Environment was a large determining factor in how early humans built their first shelters. (TF)

5. Some societies still build houses on stilts even though they no longer live in areas prone to floods. (TF)

6. In Africa today, even though they may have the same floor plan, many houses have corrugated metal instead of thatch roofs. This is an example of a modified traditional house. (TF)

7. Today, modernized traditional dwellings are the most common type found in the United States. (TF)

8. A majority of the world's people still live in villages. (TF)

9. The definition of a village varies from country to country depending on the number of inhabitants. (TF)

10. The round village developed in East Africa and had a central cattle corral. (TF)

STUDY QUESTIONS

1. List the five things a house can reveal about a region and its culture. What can be learned from the layout and function of houses?

2. Discuss the reasons for different settlement patterns. List in chronological order changes that probably occurred in housing structure since humans built their first shelters, and the probable reasons for these changes. Why is it so difficult to trace diffused building patterns?

3. Discuss the different types of building materials, where they might be found, and how they are used in relation to the environment. In today's world, why are some building materials found far from their source areas? Why are they used so far from their sources?

4. How does the function of village and farm buildings differ between the prosperous Western countries and those poorer countries where subsistence farming is widely practiced?

Notes

117

Notes

CHAPTER 20. COMMERCIALIZATION AND THE TRANSFORMATION OF THE RURAL SECTOR

CHAPTER INTRODUCTION

Agriculture is practiced in some form by virtually all of humanity, but the range and types of practices are quite different. Commercial agriculture is largely a European invention and spread with colonization and the Industrial Revolution. Development of a global transportation network to support industrialization facilitated the flow of foodstuffs to the colonial powers, who also introduced plantation agriculture in their colonies to produce luxury-crops. These systems still persist today and affect the well-being of many poorer countries. The following points should be noted when reading this chapter.

A Global Network
Modern commercial agriculture developed out of a global system of commodity exchange established by European colonial powers. As the era of global exploration and colonization by European countries unfolded, new products, both agricultural and nonagricultural, from the colonial countries became available to a European population that was both growing and becoming more affluent as a result of the Second Agricultural Revolution and the Industrial Revolution. Products from an industrializing Europe made their way to colonies around the world. Transportation between source and market was handled by the shipping fleets of the major colonial powers, producing a global pattern of raw materials, manufactured products, and foodstuffs moving between colonies and colonial powers.

Plantations
Plantations—large land holdings devoted to the efficient production of a single tropical or subtropical crop for market—were first established in the 1400s by the Portuguese on islands off the west coast of Africa. Suitable natural environments and plentiful labor led colonial powers to establish plantation and luxury-crop agriculture throughout the tropical regions. Such enterprises disrupted traditional practices of subsistence agriculture, displaced farmers, appropriated land, and generally created poverty and hardship for the indigenous population. This pattern remains today even though many plantations are owned not by colonial powers but by the governments of the countries where they are located. Their persistence is largely because poorer countries need the cash generated by these crops. Today, the greatest concentration of plantations is in the American tropics.

Rice and Wheat
Most of humanity depends upon *cereal grains* for their survival, with rice and wheat feeding well over half of the world's population. In general, these two key grain crops represent different societies. Rice, originally domesticated in tropical Asia, and still the dominant crop in the south and east realms of that continent, is grown labor intensively on small plots in poorer countries. Rice production by modern commercial methods is limited to a few countries and the cost of such production often makes it too expensive for many of the poorer countries who need it most.

Wheat, the second most important of the world's grain crops, was domesticated in several locations (see Table 20-1) and lends itself well to commercial production methods. It has come to be associated with Western cultures, where it is grown on large land holdings by mechanized means in the richer countries. The principal grain moving in international trade, it is also grown at a subsistence level by millions of farmers as a first or second crop where environmental conditions are favorable.

The Third Agricultural Revolution
Experimenting with technologically manipulated seed varieties to increase yields began in the American Midwest in the 1930s. By the 1960s, scientists in the Philippines had created a new variety of rice (called IR8) with a number of desirable characteristics and the so-called Green Revolution was born.

Coming at a time of growing concern about global hunger, the successes of the Green Revolution were truly extraordinary. While eliminating disastrous famines of the past through increased yields, the social and environmental consequences of the Green Revolution were not always benign.

In the last decade an entire field of biotechnology has sprung up in conjunction with the Third Agricultural Revolution with the development of genetically modified foods as its principal orientation. While the promise of such development in a world where almost a billion people are malnourished is evident, controversy is equally present. The concern is that gene manipulation—application of modern technology in the service of genetic modification—could create health risks and produce environmental hazards. Biotechnology can play a role in addressing the problem of hunger, but it cannot solve the problem.

CHAPTER QUIZ

MULTIPLE-CHOICE QUESTIONS

1. In which region do whole national economies depend on sugar exports.
   a. South Pacific
   b. Caribbean
   c. Pacific Rim
   d. East Africa

2. The colonial powers established cotton plantations in many different countries. Today these same countries:
   a. still export all their cotton production
   b. no longer grow any cotton
   c. have established factories to produce goods for the domestic market
   d. sell their cotton to each other instead of the developed countries

3. In 1954, the U. S. government supported the overthrow of the government of a country, possibly because of political pressure from an American multinational corporation concerned about agrarian land reforms being instituted. The country was:
   a. Mexico
   b. Cuba
   c. Haiti
   d. Guatemala

4. Today, 75 percent of the rubber produced comes from:
   a. South America
   b. Netherlands
   c. Southeast Asia
   d. lowlands of Florida

5. When the United States imposed an embargo on imports from Cuba in the 1960s, the principal Cuban export affected was:
   a. coffee
   b. cigars
   c. tea
   d. sugar

6. After petroleum, this is the second most valuable traded commodity in the world.
   a. coffee
   b. tea
   c. sugar
   d. wheat

7. The world's tea plantations are concentrated in:
   a. Africa
   b. South America
   c. Asia
   d. the Caribbean

8. The world's largest exporter of rice is:
   a. China
   b. the United States
   c. Thailand
   d. Vietnam

9. The Third Agricultural Revolution came about because of:
   a. crop diversification in developing countries
   b. governments in developing countries giving farmers more money to grow more crops
   c. biotechnology
   d. global warming

10. Over 90 percent of illegal opium comes from:
    a. Columbia and Peru
    b. Afghanistan and Myanmar
    c. Morocco and Mali
    d. Iran and Iraq

TRUE/FALSE QUESTIONS

1. Commercial agriculture has little or no effect on the environment. (TF)

2. Sugar producing and exporting countries set their own prices. (TF)

3. Cartels formed by countries producing the same produce are very successful. (TF)

4. Cotton cultivation expanded greatly during the nineteenth century because of the Industrial Revolution. (TF)

5. Lately efforts have been made to establish rubber plantations in northern Brazil. (TF)

6. In contrast to coffee, most tea is consumed in the countries where it is grown. (TF)

7. A rice plant called IR36 was the most widely grown crop on Earth in 1992. (TF)

8. The expanded use of chemical fertilizers and pesticides is no longer a concern in commercial agriculture because of new cultivation methods. (TF)

9. From the southern prairie provinces of Canada south through the United States lies an extensive wheat-growing region. (TF)

10. Grapes, olives, figs, dates, and some vegetables are grown in what is called the diversified tropical agriculture zone. (TF)

STUDY QUESTIONS

1. What are cartels and what is their purpose? Are they usually successful? Can they be used for both food and non-food commodities?

2. Explain how and why rubber production shifted from its source region. Is the rubber industry as important as it once was? Why or why not?

3. Study text Figure 20-1. Can you find climatic relationships in similar crop-growing areas around the world? If so, what does this tell you about the cultures in these regions?

4. Describe the Third Agricultural Revolution and how it has affected crop production. When did it start? Where has this revolution had its greatest impact?

5. What are genetically modified foods? Where are they grown? Why is there controversy about these foods?

Notes

Notes

PART SEVEN: THE URBANIZING WORLD

CHAPTER 21. CIVILIZATION AND URBANIZATION

CHAPTER INTRODUCTION

Cities are a relatively recent development of human culture made possible by a stable food supply. The process of urbanization intensified the concentration of humanity that had already begun with agriculture. The need for central authority, organization, and coordination of effort produced the foundations for city formation. Social stratification was followed by the emergence of government, law, and the refinement of culture. The next challenge facing humanity is the success of cities with the opportunities and problems they present in the early twenty-first century.

Virtually everywhere in the world, people are moving from the countryside to towns and cities. This migration is happening so fast that the various agencies that monitor such movements cannot agree on the pace. The problem of undependable census data and inconsistent definitions make agreement all but impossible. There is, however, agreement on one point: in the twenty-first century, the world will be predominantly urban.

Early Development
The first agricultural settlements were true villages and remained so for several thousand years. They were small and did not vary much in size and there was apparently no governmental authority beyond the village. There were no public buildings and no workshops. These *egalitarian societies* —a society that is unstratified socially and all members have equal status— persisted long after agriculture was introduced.

Urbanization and the formation of states transformed egalitarian societies into stratified, functionally specialized ones. This process occurred independently in several regions, probably first in the Fertile Crescent of Southwest Asia (see text Figures 3-2 and 21-3).

The period between about 7000 B.P. and 5000 B.P. is called the *formative era* for both the development of states and urbanization—the two obviously went hand in hand—in Southwest Asia. The egalitarian society had become a *stratified society*. Now there were priests, merchants, administrators, soldiers, farmers, and craftspeople. The city had become the focus of civilization.

Diffusion in the Mediterranean Region
Urbanization spread from Mesopotamia in several directions. On the Mediterranean island of Crete, more than 3500 years ago, Knossos was the cornerstone of a system of towns of the Minoan civilization. Ideas about city life may have reached Greece from several directions but whatever the case, during the third millennium B.P. Greece became one of the most highly urbanized areas on Earth. The ancient Greeks thus assimilated concepts of urban life from Mesopotamia as well as Minoa, and the urbanization of ancient Greece ushered in a new stage in the evolution of cities. Some 2500 years ago they had produced the most highly urbanized society of their time with a network of more than 500 cities and towns, not only on the mainland but also on the many Greek islands.

The Roman Urban System

The great majority of Greece's cities and towns were located near the Mediterranean Sea, linking peninsulas and islands. When the Romans succeeded the Greeks as rulers of the region, their empire incorporated not only the Mediterranean shores but also a large part of interior Europe and North Africa.

The ancient Romans combined local traditions with Greek customs in building an urban system that extended from Britain to Mesopotamia. The Roman *urban system* was the largest yet. The capital, Rome, was the apex of a hierarchy of settlements from small villages to large cities. A *transportation network* linked all of the urban centers of the Roman Empire together by a network of land and water routes. Efficiency was a Roman hallmark: urban places were positioned a modest distance from each other so that they could be reached in a reasonable amount of time. Some of their surface routes still serve European motorists today. The Roman road builders created a grid of communications to link the empire together.

Preindustrial Europe

Greek and Roman concepts of urbanization diffused into Western Europe, but Europe's preindustrial cities were poorly organized, unsanitary, overcrowded, and uncomfortable places to live for the majority of their inhabitants. The adage of "the good old days" hardly applies. More efficient weapons and the invention of gunpowder forced cities to develop more extensive fortifications— fortifications that could not simply be moved outward. The greater numbers of people could only be housed by building upward, and four-and-five-storied tenements began to appear. For the ordinary people, the overcrowded cities were no place to be. When the chance came, many decided to leave for America, Australia, and other parts of the world.

Urban Stages

Cities evolve in stages. The traders' mercantile city gave way to the factory-dominated manufacturing center, and the automobile enabled the evolution of the suburbanized modern city. Today's "postmodern" cities reflect the age of high technology.

CHAPTER QUIZ

MULTIPLE-CHOICE QUESTIONS

1. As early towns in a region started to grow and become interdependent a new development took place. This was the rise of the first:
   a. states
   b. identifiable specialization
   c. egalitarian societies
   d. counties

2. Stratification of society brought into being an urban elite. From them came the concept of writing and record keeping because they:
   a. were the smartest people in the cities
   b. had free time while others had to work
   c. could demand slaves write everything down
   d. owned so much they needed a method of record keeping

3. The early cities were not large by today's standards. The largest probably had populations of about:
   a. 20,000 to 25,000
   b. 30,000 to 35,000
   c. 40,000 to 45,000
   d. 10,000 to 15,000

4. By the middle of the third millennium B.P., Greece had the largest urban complex in the world. Its two leading cities were Athens and:
   a. Troy
   b. Sparta
   c. Volos
   d. Piraeus

5. The hallmark of the Roman culture was their:
   a. architecture
   b. language
   c. efficiency
   d. clothing

6. The urban tradition on the Italian peninsula prior to the Romans came from the:
   a. Etruscans
   b. Trojans
   c. Minoans
   d. Carthaginians

7. In the early decades of the Industrial Revolution, which of the following countries had a region called the "black towns" because of soot.
   a. Holland
   b. Germany
   c. France
   d. England

8. Which of the following was a common term for factory workers in the late nineteenth and early twentieth centuries:
   a. green collar
   b. blue collar
   c. white collar
   d. red collar

9. According to the United Nations' population fund, a city in which of the following countries will challenge Tokyo as the world's most populous city.
   a. Brazil
   b. Germany
   c. India
   d. United States

10. The northern boundary of the Roman Empire in Britain was marked by:
    a. Caesar's Wall
    b. the Great Wall
    c. Hadrian's Wall
    d. the Thames River

TRUE/FALSE QUESTIONS

1. The manufacturing city first emerged in the British Midlands. (TF)

2. One of the world's earliest states developed in Mesopotamia. (TF)

3. Urbanization diffused directly from Mesopotamia to Greece. (TF)

4. To link their empire together, the Romans built roads. (TF)

5. The Roman forum was used only by the elite. (TF)

6. The Chinese city of Xian was known as the Rome of East Asia. (TF)

7. Climate played a role in Europe's recovery from post-Roman decline. (TF)

8. During the fourteenth century much of Europe and many other places around the world turned colder and became drier. (TF)

9. Developed during colonial times, the mercantile city is given credit for starting a downtown area, which had not existed in towns or cities before. (TF)

10. The early manufacturing cities offered good living conditions for their citizens. (TF)

STUDY QUESTIONS

1. Discuss how small early settlements went from egalitarian societies to being stratified cities. How did this transition lead to the development of the first states?

2. What role did function and location play in the development of the early cities? What basic factors were needed?

3. Why was the urbanization of ancient Greece different from past urbanizations? How were the cities laid out? What was the quality of life in these Greek cities? How did the Romans change the Greek city and its focus?

4. Discuss the development of cities in preindustrial Europe. How did they change with the development of new weapons? What was life like in these cities?

5. What are the characteristics of the primate city?

Notes

Notes

CHAPTER 22.   LOCATION, PATTERN, AND STRUCTURE OF CITIES

CHAPTER INTRODUCTION

The study of how cities function, their internal systems and structures, and the external influences on them is the field of *urban geography*. Urban geographers want to know how cities are arranged, what they look like, how their circulation systems function, how commuting patterns develop and change, how and why people move from one part of the city to another—in short, how and why a city and its residents look, act, and change as they do. To do these studies, of course, you need to have urban places.

All cities are not equally successful. An urban center's location strongly influences its fortunes. Its position in a large and productive *hinterland*—surrounding service area—can ensure its well-being. The hinterland reveals the *economic reach* of each settlement—the maximum distance at which people are still attracted for business purposes.

Locational Factors

The answer to the question of why some urban centers are more successful than others is geography. When it comes to explaining the growth and success of certain cities, *situation*—the external locational attributes of an urban center; its relative location or regional position with reference to other nonlocal places—is often the key. A city's situation can change, and the world's largest and most enduring cities have seen their situation improve with the times. Conversely, a city's situation can also deteriorate over time. Exhaustion of resources, repeated crop failures, climatic change, and political developments all can change a city's situation.

A second locational factor affecting the development of cities and towns is their *site*—the actual physical qualities of the place a city occupies. An urban center's site may have played a key role in its original and early survival, for example, as a defensive locale; but in modern times that same site may limit its growth and expansion. Air stagnation, depleted water supplies, or changes in transportation routes and means can reduce a previously advantageous site to a liability.

Spatial Organization

The Industrial Revolution occurred almost a century later in the United States than in Europe. When it finally did cross the Atlantic in the 1870s, it progressed so robustly that only 50 years later America surpassed Europe as the world's mightiest industrial power.

The impact of industrial urbanization was felt at two levels. At the national level, there quickly emerged a network of cities specialized in the collection, processing, and distribution of raw materials and manufactured goods, and linked together by an even more efficient web of transport routes. The whole process unfolded so quickly that planning was impossible. Almost literally, near the turn of the twentieth century America awoke to discover that it had built a number of large cities.

In the United States, the urban system evolved through five stages of development determined by prevailing modes of transport and industry. Today's period of high technology, still in the process of transforming the modern city, dates from the 1970s.

Urban Structure

Cities are not simply random collections of buildings and people. They exhibit *functional structure*: they are spatially organized to perform their functions as places of commerce, production, education, and much more. Throughout the past century urban geographers have attempted to construct models that would account for the geographic layout of cities (see text Figure 22-5). The task grew more complicated as manufacturing cities became modern cities and modern cities became postmodern. Today, urban geographers identify superregions that they call urban realms, and they create models that show cities within cities (text Figure 22-6).

Models of urban structure reveal how the forces that shape the internal layout of cities have changed, transforming the single-center city with one dominant downtown into the polycentric metropolis with several commercial nodes.

Urban Functions

Every urban center has an economic base, with some workers employed in *basic* (that is, goods-producing) sectors that satisfy demand in the hinterland or markets even farther away. These activities produce goods for export and generate an inflow of money. On the other hand, workers who maintain city streets, clerks who work in offices, and teachers who teach in city schools are responsible for the functions of the city itself. This is the *nonbasic* (also called the service) sector. Some people who work in a city, of course, do some of each. A mechanic may serve customers from a village in the city's hinterland, where there are no repair facilities, while also serving city residents.

This employment structure—the number of people employed in various basic and nonbasic jobs—reveals the primary functions a city performs. You should note that all cities have multiple functions, and the larger the city, the larger the number of functions. Some cities, however, are dominated by one particular activity. This *functional specialization* was a characteristic of European cities even before the Industrial Revolution, but the Industrial Revolution gave it new meaning. This was once true in America as well, as text Figure 22-8 reveals, but the situation revealed in these three maps no longer exists, at least to the extent shown on the maps. As urban centers grow, they tend to lose their specialization.

Central Places

The notion of a *hierarchy* of urban places, discussed earlier, identifies urban settlements ranging from hamlets to metropolises and is based not only on population but also on functions and services. These functions and services attract customers from both the urban areas and areas beyond the urban limits. Thus every urban center has a certain *economic reach* that can be used as a measure of its centrality—the strength of an urban center is its capacity to attract producers and consumers to its facilities.

In 1933, Walter Christaller laid the groundwork for *central place theory*. Christaller attempted to develop a model that would show how and where central places in the urban hierarchy (hamlets, villages, towns, and cities) would be functionally distributed, based on their respective provision of *central goods and services*—goods and services that a central place makes available to its consumers in a surrounding region—as opposed to those universally available. While not totally applicable in the real world, central place theory helps to explain why, under ideal circumstances, small urban places such as villages lie closer together while larger cities lie far apart.

CHAPTER QUIZ

MULTIPLE-CHOICE QUESTIONS

1. The area surrounding a village or town that depends on that urban place for services is called the:
    a. boondocks
    b. hinterland
    c. support region
    d. rural area

2. In ranking urban places, which of the following is at the bottom of the urban hierarchy.
    a. town
    b. hamlet
    c. village
    d. suburb

3. In some parts of the world, large metropolises are coalescing to create megacities called megalopolises. One such is the so-called Bosnywash in the United States. It is located:
    a. in southern Texas
    b. around Puget Sound in the Pacific Northwest
    c. on the Eastern Slope of the Rocky Mountains
    d. along the U.S. Northeast Coast

4. In the early twenty-first century, the world's fastest-growing urban area is:
    a. Shenzhen
    b. Hong Kong
    c. Mexico City
    d. Tokyo

5. The city of Paris is located on which of the following rivers.
    a. Rhine
    b. Thames
    c. Seine
    d. Marne

6. The capital city of Thailand has some of the most polluted air in the world. This city is:
    a. Singapore
    b. Gung How
    c. Djakarta
    d. Bangkok

7. The *Iron Horse Epoch* of the evolution of the American urban system was dominated by the diffusion of the:
    a. steel industry
    b. automobile
    c. steam boat
    d. steam-powered railroad

8. The rank-size rule of urban places does not apply in countries with:
   a. dominant primate cities
   b. very long coast lines
   c. mainly urban populations
   d. Interstate Highway Systems

9. In metropolitan Los Angeles, how many discrete urban realms have emerged around the central city.
   a. eight
   b. seven
   c. six
   d. five

10. In the 1940s, retail centers in America were concentrated in which of the following regions.
    a. the Northeast
    b. the South
    c. the Great Plains
    d. the West Coast

TRUE/FALSE QUESTIONS

1. In today's world, some regional cities are so successful and powerful that their leaders can afford to do business directly with foreign countries. (TF)

2. While some hamlets may have no urban functions, villages are likely to. (TF)

3. The megalopolis of Bosnywash in the United States has a global economic reach. (TF)

4. Workers in manufacturing plants work in the nonbasic sector. (TF)

5. In a city, the number of nonbasic workers is never greater than the number of basic workers. (TF)

6. Detroit has long been the dominant city of the North American interior. (TF)

7. Christaller's central place theory was never proven to fit any place in the world. (TF)

9. When it comes to explaining the growth and success of certain cities, site often is the key. (TF)

10. Functional specialization was not a characteristic of European cities before the Industrial Revolution. (TF)

STUDY QUESTIONS

1. List and define the ranking system for urban places. What is a hinterland and why is it important?

2. List the positive and negative factors found in and around a city's site. Do the same for a city's relative location (situation). Give two example cities and explain how these factors have affected them. Have their relative locations (situations) changed over time?

3. Explain the rank-size rule. Where doesn't this rule apply?

4. Explain the difference between basic and nonbasic sectors. Give examples of jobs in each and their role in the urban environment.

5. When we talk about the primary functions of an urban place today, why is functional specialization no longer so important?

6. What was Christaller's main contribution to geography?

Notes

Notes

Notes

CHAPTER 23.　　　GLOBAL URBANIZATION

CHAPTER INTRODUCTION

The urban influences affecting the cultural geography of the modern world represent the end of a long evolutionary process resulting from the influences of different cultures with their goals and capabilities.

A city, regardless of the culture where it develops, represents society, culture, opportunity, success, and failure. Europe and America are urbanized societies whose cities and cultures are changing within an urban environment, a condition not true in the developing world. The growing cities and urban places of the developing world represent the greatest challenge to traditional cultures in the early twenty-first century. Developing societies face the formidable task of retaining their cultural identities and traditional values in a rapidly changing world. On their success or failure rests the successful existence of much of humanity.

Demographers estimate two centuries ago less than 5 percent of the world's population was urbanized. Today the figure approaches 50 percent and some regional differences and changes are striking, such as in the developing world, which will hold the 23 largest cities within 15 years. In some parts of the world, megalopolises are evolving from formerly separate cities. In others, megacities are emerging with populations that exceed those of many countries. In this chapter we will discuss these regional changes and focus on several of the critical problems rapid urbanization has produced. As you will see, the problems of large cities are cross-cultural; they differ in degree, not in kind.

Colonial Legacies

South America, Southeast Asia, and Sub-Saharan Africa share a common imprint in their colonial heritage. Everywhere that urbanization is occurring, there is the imprint of the colonial era alongside the traditional culture. In these three realms, cities reflect their colonial beginnings as well as more recent domestic developments. In South and Middle America the fastest growth is where Iberian cultures dominate. Southeast Asian urban centers are growing rapidly, with foreign influences and investments continuing to play a dominant role. In African cities, the diversity caused by European influence in some, and decided the lack of it in others, makes it difficult to formulate a model African city that would account for all or even most of what is there.

World Urbanization

As a percentage of total population, urban dwellers are most numerous in the core areas of Western Europe, North America, Japan, and Australia. There are also remarkably high percentages of urbanization in several countries in the periphery (text Figure 23-1). In addition, urbanization is currently occurring rapidly in many peripheral countries, especially in Sub-Saharan Africa. This region has both the lowest percentage of its population classed as urban **and** the fastest growing urban population in the world. In the western hemisphere, taking 70 percent and higher as the highest category, Mexico and Cuba are on a par with France, and Mexico's level of urbanization is higher than that of several Eastern European countries.

The culturally and economically diverse realm of Southwest Asia and North Africa displays remarkable variation in levels of urbanization. This variation is related to differences in national economics and cultures. Much of the realm, the Middle East and the Arabian Peninsula, is quite highly urbanized. *Nucleation* resulting from the oil industry has much to do with this situation.

Urbanization in South Asia remains low. For the realm as a whole, urbanization remains well below 30 percent. Southeast Asia, as a realm, is marked by low levels of urbanization (the city-state of Singapore is 100 percent urban; the only such country in the world). As a whole, East Asia is only about 36 percent urban, despite the rapid economic growth on the western Pacific Rim.

The Great Cities

More than 300 cities in the world have populations exceeding 1 million (text Figure 23-3). If you compare this map with text Figure 23-2, you will find that the former map shows the concentration of large cities in eastern North America, Western Europe, and Japan. Several of the great urban complexes in these regions are the products of megalopolitan coalescence. The fastest-growing megacities, however, are in South and East Asia.

Table 23-1 shows that many of the world's most populous cities are found in the poorer countries, and it also indicates how fast individual cities in poorer countries are growing compared to conurbations in richer countries. Despite wretched living conditions for many of their inhabitants, cities continue to attract new residents by the millions.

CHAPTER QUIZ

MULTIPLE-CHOICE QUESTIONS

1. The outer ring in both Latin American cities and Southeast Asian cities is usually the place where:
    a. slums and squatter settlements are located
    b. the rich live
    c. markets are found
    d. the industrial area is located

2. In African cities vertical growth occurs mainly in the __?__ part of the city.
    a. outer
    b. old colonial CBD
    c. transitional business center
    d. native CBD

3. Which of the following continents has the lowest level of urbanization.
    a. Australia
    b. Africa
    c. South America
    d. Asia

4. Outside North America and Western Europe, major megalopolitan development is occurring only in which of the following.
    a. China
    b. Australia
    c. Japan
    d. India

5. Cities in poorer parts of the world generally lack enforceable laws to ensure the orderly use of space. Such laws are called ? laws.
   a. planning
   b. economic
   c. zoning
   d. population control

6. United Nations studies suggest that by 2035 there may be as many as ? cities with populations over 20 million.
   a. 15
   b. 20
   c. 25
   d. 30

7. In early 2002, the fastest-growing megacities in the world are in:
   a. South and East Asia
   b. Western Europe and Japan
   c. Eastern North America
   d. Central and South America

8. In 1950, the only city in the world with more than 10 million residents was:
   a. London
   b. Paris
   c. Tokyo
   d. New York

9. Nucleation resulting from ? has resulted in the Southwest Asian and North African realm, the Middle East, and the Arabian Peninsula being highly urbanized.
   a. irrigation water
   b. a strategic location
   c. the oil industry
   d. new high-tech industries

10. The world's tallest buildings are located in:
   a. Brazil
   b. Malaysia
   c. Australia
   d. France

TRUE/FALSE QUESTIONS

1. The African city quite often contains three central business districts. (TF)

2. The cities of South and Middle America are so similar in development and layout that almost any model of a modern city can represent all their aspects. (TF)

3. According to the United Nations Population Fund, the African city of Lagos will soon rank as the world's third largest in population. (TF)

4. In the early twenty-first century, cities with a million or more inhabitants can be counted in the hundreds. (TF)

5. During the 1990s, Europe had the world's fastest-growing cities. (TF)

6. Many of the world's evolving megacities are located in the less prosperous parts of the world. (TF)

7 The whole urbanized area of Europe extends over an area about half the size of the entire United States. (TF)

8. The three countries of the South American "cone" are Argentina, Chile, and Uruguay. (TF)

9. By 2015, not one of the world's 23 most populous cities will be a European city. (TF)

10. Rosario is Argentina's primate city. (TF)

STUDY QUESTIONS

1. Table 23-1 makes clear that the pattern of world urbanization is undergoing dramatic change. List some of the reasons that the old pattern where European cities were always the largest will no longer be the case. Where will the future megacities be located and why?

2. Discuss urbanization by continent and region using text Figure 23-2 and the material in your text. Also look at text Figure 23-3 and find the countries with the largest cities. Relating back to the text, which cities are growing the fastest? Which regions have the slowest-growing cities? Why is this pattern emerging?

3. List the factors that make cities in Latin America, Southeast Asia, and Africa different from American and European cities. What is the prime reason these cities developed differently?

Notes

Notes

PART EIGHT: THE ROOTS AND CONSEQUENCES OF INDUSTRIALIZATION

CHAPTER 24.   INDUSTRIAL ACTIVITY AND GEOGRAPHIC LOCATION

CHAPTER OUTLINE

The Industrial Revolution was essentially a revolution in power and transportation. Goods, ideas, and humanity were transported across the Earth in a manner that would forever change our planet and its human occupants. Modern industry increased and intensified regional inequality while mushrooming demand for resources created new global patterns of movement. In the industrial-oriented world of the early twenty-first century success depends on the possession or control of resources. At a time when cultural differences should be reduced with benefits and technical capabilities shared for the good of all, our own innovations and abilities may work to hinder this end.

Location
Economic activities can be categorized according to their purpose, their relationship to the natural resources on which they are based, and their complexity. Economic geographers investigate the reasons behind the location of economic activity. Today, the world is a vast panorama of primary activity within which there are clusters of secondary industries symbolized by the great manufacturing belts of Japan, the United States, Europe, and Russia. What geographic factors created this arrangement and what will happen next? Answers to such questions come from the field of *location theory*, which attempts to explain the locational pattern of an economic activity in terms of the factors that influence this pattern. Location theory helps explain the spatial positioning of industries and their success or failure. The Industrial Revolution transformed the world's economic map, dramatically impacting certain areas while totally bypassing others. Understanding the forces and factors that shaped the world's industrial layout is a prime objective of economic geographers.

Location Decision
Industrial activity takes place in certain locations and not others. For primary industries, the location of resources is the determining factor. *Secondary industries* are less dependent on resource location because raw materials can be transported to distant locations if the resulting profits outweigh the costs. Any attempt to establish a model for the location of secondary industries, however, runs into complications because the location of secondary industries depends to a large extent on human behavior and decision making, cultural and political as well as economic factors, even on intuition or whim. In 1909, the German economist Alfred Weber developed a model for the location of manufacturing establishments. Weber's *least cost theory* accounted for the location of a manufacturing plant in terms of transportation (the most important), labor, and agglomeration (shared talents, services, and facilities). Despite numerous criticisms of the model, Alfred Weber set in motion a debate over the spatial aspects of economic activity that continues today.

Transportation

As Weber noted, *transportation* facilities and costs are crucial in industrial location. A huge market may exist for a given product, but if that market is not served by an effective transportation system, much of the advantage is lost. The maps in Chapter 25 underscore the fact that highly developed industrial areas are also the places that are served most efficiently by transportation facilities. Industrialization and the development of modern transport systems go hand-in-hand.

In a sense, the Industrial Revolution was a transportation revolution—a revolution that is still going on. Transport costs played a key role in the location of heavy industries but raw-material acquisition and finished-product distribution determined the options. One of the first decisions faced by the capitalists who built the great iron works of Europe, for example, was whether to move coal to iron ores sites or iron ore to the coal fields. The iron smelters were built near the coal fields (it generally takes more coal than iron ore to make a ton of finished product). The same decision was made when the American iron industry located near Appalachian coal and hauled iron ore from the Great Lakes Mesabi Range.

Additional Factors of Location

Other factors influencing the location of industries include labor costs, energy availability, and infrastructure. The availability of cheap semiskilled labor has had an immense impact on regional industrial development. Even in an era of automated assembly lines and computerized processing, the prospect of a large, low-wage, trainable labor force continues to attract manufacturers. Japan's postwar success was based in large measure on the skills *and* the low wages of its labor force. Taiwan and South Korea have successfully competed with Japan for the same reason. In the 1980s, China entered the Pacific Rim picture with its huge labor force and will, in turn, feel the impact of cheap labor when Vietnam enters the picture. The cost of labor still looms large in the location of industry.

The availability of an *energy* supply, another factor in the location of industry, used to be much more important than it is today. The early British textile mills were "site-tied" because they depended on falling water to drive the looms. Today, power comes from different sources and can be transmitted or transported over long distances. Exceptions occur when an industry needs very large amounts of energy, for example, certain metallurgical and chemical industries.

When Weber considered the role of agglomeration in location decisions, he could not foresee the dimensions of urban areas or industrial complexes a century hence. One of the most difficult problems that today's industrializing countries or regions face is providing adequate *infrastructure* —transportation and communication networks, banks, postal service, administrative assistance, energy distribution systems, social services, roads and highways. China has tried to slow industrialization in some regions because of an inadequate infrastructure. Thus many factors of industrial location are not accounted for by models. Even the growth of secondary industries is influenced by factors that are not accounted for in the models, such as political changes and even environmental fluctuations.

CHAPTER QUIZ

MULTIPLE-CHOICE QUESTIONS

1. In 1721, British textile makers rioted to protest the importation of foreign-made textiles from:
   a. India
   b. Egypt
   c. Japan
   d. Hong Kong

2. Before the Industrial Revolution, European industrial products suffered from:
   a. a lack of raw material
   b. depressed prices
   c. tariffs
   d. poor quality

3. The first steps in the Industrial Revolution involved:
   a. improved food supplies
   b. the use of electricity
   c. better machines
   d. importing foreign laborers

4. Weber's least cost theory accounts for the location of a manufacturing plant by considering which of the following to be the most important.
   a. power
   b. transportation
   c. raw material
   d. labor

5. The current economic boom on the Pacific Rim is based largely on:
   a. transportation advantages
   b. power supplies
   c. market proximity
   d. labor costs

6. The term *Black Towns* was applied to early industrial towns in the:
   a. British Midlands
   b. Ruhr in Germany
   c. Po Valley in Italy
   d. Saar region

7. The location of steel plants in which part of the United States was influenced by the need to import iron ore from overseas sources.
   a. the Ohio River Valley
   b. the Southern Appalachians

147

c. the northeastern seaboard
d. the Pacific Northwest

8. Which of the following Asian countries, using the example of Britain's control of the sources of industrial raw material through colonization, followed a similar path of colonial expansion.
    a. China
    b. Japan
    c. India
    d. Thailand

9. In a sense, the Industrial Revolution was a revolution in:
    a. power sources
    b. technological application
    c. labor utilization
    d. transportation

10. For most industrial goods, which method of transport is cheapest over short distances.
    a. truck
    b. railroad
    c. barge
    d. ships

TRUE/FALSE QUESTIONS

1. Hong Kong could have developed a superior economy based on primary industry. (TF)

2. No industries of any kind existed before the Industrial Revolution. (TF)

3. Transportation, not location, is the determining factor for primary industries. (TF)

4. In Weber's least cost theory, transportation and labor availability play a large role. (TF)

5. In the United States, steel mills are located along the northeastern seaboard because they use imported iron ore. (TF)

6. Colonization did **not** give the controlling countries access to many raw materials. (TF)

7. When labor in Japan began to cost more, Taiwan and South Korea surged ahead in the production and export of low-cost products. (TF)

8. Certain industries will generally shift from country to country as long as low cost labor is available. (TF)

9. China has tried to slow the rate of industrialization on the Pacific Rim because of a lack of available raw materials. (TF)

10. A close source of energy is necessary for industrial development. (TF)

STUDY QUESTIONS

1. Why is it accurate to describe the world today as being in the modern age of industrial intensification? Did the Industrial Revolution affect all regions in Europe? Why or why not?

2. Why are secondary industries less dependent on resource location? What factors are taken into account in site location?

3. Describe Weber's least cost theory.

4. List and describe the factors that are considered in industrial site location. Why is Japan a prime example of the role of transportation with relationship to industrialization?

Notes

Notes

Notes

CHAPTER 25.   RESOURCES AND REGIONS: THE GLOBAL DISTRIBUTION OF INDUSTRY

CHAPTER INTRODUCTION

The future of today's world is being shaped by industrialization. The remarkable achievements that began in a single nation have not yet been shared equally by all humanity but this may be about to change. Modern industry is largely a phenomenon of countries in the mid-latitudes of the Northern Hemisphere with few peripheral countries as yet members of this rather exclusive club. In the early twenty-first century much has changed concerning industrialization and the resources that support it. Industry is presently undergoing a global shift that portends a new era for the world as we have come to know it.

When the Bolsheviks took control of the Russian Empire, they found themselves in charge of a vast realm with a mainly agricultural economy. There was nothing in the Soviet Union of the 1920s to rival what was happening in Europe or North America. Soviet communist rulers were determined to change this. They wanted to transform the Soviet economy into an industrial one. The human cost of this gigantic scheme was dreadful, but the desired transformation was accomplished. The Soviet Union became a major industrial power with vast manufacturing complexes.

Outside the Soviet Union, industrial development took a very different course. Market forces, not state planning, propelled the Industrial Revolution in Europe and North America, and industrial economies on both sides of the Atlantic Ocean rose to global prominence. For more than four decades after World War II, Eastern Europe's industrial development was constrained by the imposition of Soviet ideology and economic planning. Western Europe's industrial growth proceeded more freely, and in the postwar period Japan, Taiwan, and South Korea industrialized under free-enterprise rules as well. China, on the other hand, collectivized its agriculture and put its industries under state control.

Major Industrial Regions

Whatever the ideological basis (market-commercial, communist-state, or some combination), the world map of major regional-industrial development reveals that only a small minority of countries have become major industrial economies. Four major industrial regions have developed, all in the Northern Hemisphere: Western and Central Europe (text Figure 25-1), Eastern North America (text Figure 25-3), Russia-Ukraine (text Figure 25-4), and Eastern Asia (text Figure 25-5). Each consists of core areas with subsidiary clusters some distance away.

While the older manufacturing regions are quite entrenched, notable shifts are occurring. This dispersal is especially evident in East Asia, where Japan's dominance has been challenged by the "Four Tigers" of East Asia. In addition, the entrance of China into the global manufacturing economy in the 1980s is certain to gain in significance in the twenty-first century.

Europe

The location of Europe's primary industrial regions still reflects the spatial diffusion of the Industrial Revolution. An axis of manufacturing extends from Britain to Poland and the Czech Republic, and onward to Ukraine. The explanation of this pattern lies in the location of coal fields in Britain and the European continent. Britain's coal-fired industries produced a pattern of functional specialization that for a time had no equal in the world, for it was coal that fired the Industrial Revolution.

153

Europe's coal deposits lie in a belt across northern France, Belgium, north-central Germany, the northwestern Czech Republic, and southern Poland. When the Industrial Revolution diffused from Britain onto the mainland it was along this zone that Europe's major concentrations of heavy industry developed. Europe's industrial success also depended on the skills of its labor force and the high degree of specialization achieved in various industrial zones.

North America
North American manufacturing rapidly developed, occurring first in the east. Development was served by a wide array of natural resources and supported by networks of natural as well as artificial transportation systems. All were remote from the destruction caused by wars, and on the doorstep of the world's richest market. Today, this complex, anchored by the American Manufacturing Belt—from the northeastern seaboard to Iowa, and from the St. Lawrence Valley to the confluence of the Ohio and Mississippi Rivers—is the largest in the world (text Figure 25-3).

The Former Soviet Union
The most important country detached from the Soviet Empire (after Russia itself) was Ukraine. In the new Europe, Ukraine would be the largest territorial state and one of the most populous. It was a major manufacturing center before the end of the nineteenth century, having been strongly affected by the Industrial Revolution. Coal from its Donetsk Basin (Donbas) and iron ore from the Krivoy Rog reserve and later from Russia's Kursk Magnetic Anomaly allowed Ukraine to grow into one of the world's largest manufacturing complexes. Today, despite Ukraine's political separation from the former Soviet Union (and hence from Russia), Ukrainian and Russian industries are inter-dependent: Ukraine needs Russian fuels and Russia needs Ukrainian raw materials.

Eastern Asia
Two centuries after the onset of the Industrial Revolution, East Asia is the cauldron of industrialization. From Japan to Guangdong and from South Korea to Singapore, the islands, countries, provinces, and cities fronting the Pacific Ocean are caught up in a frenzy of industrialization that has made the term *Pacific Rim* synonymous with economic opportunity. Industrial regions in East Asia are the fastest growing in the world. The Asian Pacific Rim, from Japan to Indonesia, includes several of the most rapidly expanding economies, recent setbacks notwithstanding.

CHAPTER QUIZ

MULTIPLE-CHOICE QUESTIONS

1. Which of the following is **not** a major industrial region
   a. East Asia
   b. South Asia
   c. Western Europe
   d. Russia

2. When the Industrial Revolution spread to mainland Europe, it first took root in southern Belgium, where __?__ were available.
   a. good transportation and labor
   b. oil and gas

c. coal and iron

d. railroad connections and port facilities

3. The key resources on which twentieth-century industrialization was built were:
   a. coal and iron ore
   b. coal and oil
   c. iron ore and natural gas
   d. oil and natural gas

4. The United States is one of the world's largest __?__ producers.
   a. coal
   b. petroleum
   c. oil shale
   d. hydroelectric

5. Countries with large reserves of oil and natural gas occupy a special position in the global economic picture. Currently, the only one of these that is a major industrial power is:
   a. Saudi Arabia
   b. Russia
   c. Venezuela
   d. Iraq

6. Concerns over the long-term implications of a decline in oil reserves have led Kuwait to seek an alternative source of wealth. This source is:
   a. potable water
   b. coal
   c. shipping
   d. agriculture

7. After WW I Ukraine produced as much as __?__ percent of all coal mined in the then Soviet Union.
   a. 55
   b. 70
   c. 80
   d. 90

8. One of Russia's oldest thriving manufacturing areas is:
   a. the Volga
   b. Urals
   c. St. Petersburg
   d. Vladivostok

9. Japan's dominant region of industrialization and urbanization is the:
   a. Kansai District
   b. Kanto Plain
   c. Kitakyushu District
   d. Toyama District

10. Among the Four Tigers, which has emerged as the largest industrial power.
    a. Hong Kong
    b. Taiwan
    c. Singapore
    d. South Korea

TRUE/FALSE QUESTIONS

1. The global distribution of industry can be understood solely by reference to the types of variables highlighted by Weber. (TF)

2. Britain was the first world nation to industrialize. (TF)

3. New York is one of the world's major break-of-bulk locations. (TF)

4. The U. S. dependency on foreign oil is very low. (TF)

5. Currently, all four of the world's principal industrial regions that developed during the mid-twentieth century depend on external fuel supplies. (TF)

6. When the world's oil supply runs out, it will be the oil-producing countries themselves that will face the greatest adjustments. (TF)

7. Japan's northern most island is Honshu. (TF)

8. Until the early 1960s, China's communist-era industrial development was aided by Soviet planners. (TF)

9. Japan has three major industrial areas. (TF)

10. China's coastal areas are industrializing, but the process shows signs of having run its course in Japan. (TF)

STUDY QUESTIONS

1. When you look at text Figure 25-1, what do almost all of Europe's industrial and urban areas have in common? Read the text. Which regions lie on coal fields? Besides resources, what other factors help to create the industrial regions?

2. Referring to text Figures 25-2 and 25-3, can you find a correlation between the location of fossil fuel and manufacturing regions? Is energy readily available in the major manufacturing belt? Identify the other manufacturing areas and what they produce. What are maquiladora plants, where are they located, and what do they produce?

3. Looking at text Figure 25-4, what connects all of Russia's manufacturing regions? List the regions and some of their products.

4. Identify manufacturing regions in East Asia and their products using text Figure 25-5. Where is the Pacific Rim? What do these regions produce? How are they changing?

Notes

Notes

Notes

CHAPTER 26.   CONCEPTS OF DEVELOPMENT

CHAPTER INTRODUCTION

In the last 200 years the benefits and influences of industrialization have spread, in varying degrees, to all parts of the Earth. In many countries this process has produced intraregional contrasts that tend to intensify the contrasts between urban and rural populations. This development is, unfortunately, often more symbolic than real for many countries and actually helps these societies very little. Industrialization is not the solution for many countries seeking to improve conditions for their citizens. Success is measured in many ways but should be judged based on criteria and achievement applicable to the society involved. In the twenty-first century poorer, less industrialized countries must balance goals and ambitions with the needs of their populations.

Patterns of Development

The global economic picture is characterized by enormous gaps between rich and poor countries, but the geography of economic well-being also reveals regional disparities within countries at all levels of development. There are even areas within the industrialized countries themselves where change is slow in coming. Parts of the rural South in the United States still experience significant poverty and remain comparatively remote from the effects of national economic growth. Life has changed little in remote areas of western and northern Japan, and areas of isolation and stagnation persist in Europe.

In poorer, less industrialized countries there are places where clusters of industries have emerged and rapid urban growth is taking place, producing local conditions that differ sharply from those prevailing in surrounding areas. Recent economic growth on the Pacific Rim of East Asia has created huge regional disparities in economic conditions between some coastal provinces of China and distant interior provinces. Such regional contrasts have significant as well as political consequences. Regional economic disparities are increasing throughout the world.

Concepts and Approaches

Economists and geographers use a variety of approaches to describe the wide disparities in the global economy. Countries with high levels of urbanization and industrialization and high standards of living have long been referred to as *developed countries* (DCs), in contrast to *underdeveloped countries* (UDCs). This approach divides the world into two major categories, but also assumes that all countries are at some stage of development. But, the concept of development is a complicated one. How, for example, should development be measured? The GNP index provides one approach, but it has many shortcomings. There are a number of things it does not measure, such as the informal economy and contrasts within countries. Other approaches provide a richer basis for thinking about development, but none of these approaches produces a clear dividing line between developed and underdeveloped countries. Since some countries that were classed as under-developed began to change, the term *developing country* came into use in the 1960s and 1970s, but problems still existed, not the least of which was that no country wanted to be classed as "underdeveloped," and with good reason. The definition came from developed countries. Thus the developed–underdeveloped distinction was largely replaced by a developed–developing distinction. What all this showed is that while economic disparities are usually thought to be due to different levels of development, in reality development is much more complex and cannot be reduced to simple categories.

The Core–Periphery Model

Because of many criticisms and shortcomings in the "traditional" divisions of developed, developing, and underdeveloped systems, a new approach to describing global economic disparities has been proposed. The new one is more sensitive to geographical differences and the relationships among development processes occurring in different places. The proposed *core–periphery model*, which is also used in discussions of political power, views the world as characterized by a *core*, *semiperiphery*, and *periphery*. Since the model focuses attention on the economic relationships among places, it is a key component of many theories that treat the global economy as a large system, and is actually quite different from the developed, developing, and underdeveloped approach. The most important difference is the explicit identification of the power relationships among places, and it does not assume that socioeconomic change will occur in the same way in all places. This is important, because underlying economic disparities is a core–periphery relationship among different regions of the world. This affects how economies develop in both the core and the periphery.

A Changing World

In the early part of the twenty-first century, some states are still subsistence based and poor (*traditional*), whereas others are in the *takeoff* stage. These terms are part of a theory proposed by economist Walt Rostow in the 1960s, referred to as the *modernization model*. Rostow's model suggests that all countries follow a similar path through five stages of development. The model pro-vides a useful view of how certain parts of the world have changed over time. It has been criticized because it does not take into account the different constraints that regions face because it suggests a single development path that is not influenced by cultural differences. In today's world, development is taking place under widely different political systems. It is often associated with democratization, but it is also occurring under authoritarian regimes. We should remember that there are many routes to development.

CHAPTER QUIZ

MULTIPLE-CHOICE QUESTIONS

1. The world's fourth most populous country is:
   a. India
   b. Canada
   c. Indonesia
   d. the Philippines

2. The core–periphery model focuses attention on the __?__ relationships among places.
   a. social
   b. economic
   c. military
   d. political

3. The World Bank groups states into four categories based on income. Which of the following is **not** one of the regions where low-income countries are **concentrated**.
   a. Africa
   b. South Asia
   c. East Asia
   d. South America

4. According to World Bank statistics, there are how many middle-income countries.
   a. 45
   b. 55
   c. 65
   d. 75

5. Europe laid the foundation for its colonial expansion and global economic domination by the middle of which century.
   a. eighteenth
   b. sixteenth
   c. seventeenth
   d. nineteenth

6. Which of the following statements is correct concerning the world economic system.
   a. It works to the advantage of the periphery countries.
   b. It works to the disadvantage of periphery countries.
   c. It works to the advantage of both the core and periphery countries.
   d. It works to the disadvantage of the core countries.

7. Geographically, peripheral countries tend to be marked by:
   a. good regional developmental balance
   b. good site locations
   c. severe regional disparities
   d. good situation locations

8. In the *modernization model* of economic development as formulated by Walt Rostow, when a country reaches the *drive to maturity* stage, a majority of workers enter what sector of the economy.
   a. extractive
   b. service
   c. industrial
   d. managerial

9. In the world today, communism remains in control in three countries. Which of the following is **not** one of them.
   a. Cuba
   b. China
   c. Panama
   d. North Korea

10. In the early twenty-first century, which of the following was **not** a low-income Western Hemisphere country.
    a. Ecuador
    b. Haiti
    c. Guyana
    d. Nicaragua

TRUE/FALSE QUESTIONS

1. In all the rich, developed nations pockets of extreme poverty still exist. (TF)

2. The GNP provides the best and least controversial approach for describing the wide disparities in the global economy. (TF)

3. Gross national product figures for countries are not completely accurate because they leave out some sources of income. (TF)

4. The core–periphery model focuses on the economic relationships among places. (TF)

5. Middle-income states outnumber the poorer states. (TF)

6. The periphery countries cannot legitimately accuse developed countries of neocolonialism. (TF)

7. Tourism has been very beneficial to periphery countries by helping the poor. (TF)

8. The modernization model proposes that countries in the drive to maturity stage have sustained growth taking hold. (TF)

9. When many developing countries tried to adopt the communist state control method of economics the results were most often disastrous. (TF)

10. Politics and economics go hand-in-hand. (TF)

STUDY QUESTIONS

1. Why do you think there are such regional economic differences within a country?

2. Why are the seven measures of development suggested as alternatives for measuring economic development hard to apply in some countries?

3. Describe the core–periphery model. How is it different from other models? Study text Figure 26-1. List the conditions that put countries in the periphery. How do their industries differ in kind and dimension from core countries?

4. How does tourism affect the poorer countries? What contrasts are found?

5. List and explain the different models of development. Give some of the strong and weak points of each, if given. Do you think any one covers all the problems in deciding the development stage of a country? List some factors that helped or hindered a country in its economic development.

Notes

Notes

PART NINE: FROM DEINDUSTRIALIZATION TO GLOBALIZATION

CHAPTER 27. DEINDUSTRIALIZATION AND THE RISE OF THE SERVICE SECTOR

CHAPTER INTRODUCTION

Ever since the Industrial Revolution, the growing demand for resources, the expansion of manufacturing and trade, and technological innovation have worked to produce an increasingly interconnected global economy. Almost all places are in some way part of the web of production, exchange, and consumption that make up that economy—and their position in that web has significant social consequences. Those in the developed core tend to be in the driver's seat, whereas those in the periphery have far less control. Tracing the historical geography of industrialization can tell us much about why some areas are in a more advantageous position that others, but that is not the entire story.

Changing Patterns

The declining cost of transportation and communication, along with changes in the production process, have led to an enormous expansion of the service sector (activities such as transportation, banking, retailing, administration, and decision making are some examples). Its activities do not generate an actual tangible product. This transition has primarily occurred in the industrialized core. The service sector is sometimes broken down into three categories: tertiary, quaternary, and quinary industries. Over the past 35 years this growth in service-related activities has been accompanied by significant deindustrialization in the core industrial economies. This shift had its roots in dramatic decreases in the cost of transporting goods, the increasing mechanization of production, the growth of the public sector, and the rise of new information and communication technologies.

The changes of the past three-plus decades have not fundamentally altered global patterns of economic well-being, but they have produced significant new spatial orders. They have caused shifts in the locus of production, altered patterns of regional specialization, and fostered new centers of economic growth. Deindustrialization in the core has also led to the growth of labor-intensive manufacturing in the periphery where labor costs are dramatically lower and profits thus higher. Such manufacturing ranges from shoes and apparel to computers, automobiles, and television sets. The next time you purchase such items, check and see where they were manufactured or assembled.

Global Dimensions of Economic Activity

To understand the economic shifts that have occurred over the past few decades we must look beyond individual places to the global scale, for both the core and periphery have been significantly changed. The phrase *new international division of labor* refers to the set of relationships that define the contemporary world economy. Whereas earlier in the twentieth century economic relation-ships were defined by an industrialized core and a resource-exporting periphery, today the geog-raphy of the global economy is far more complex. The countries and regions outside the core that have increased their manufacturing output most rapidly in recent decades are shown in text Figure 27-1. Lying behind the patterns shown is a set of developments that give meaning to

167

the phrase "new international division of labor." In the traditional core, the shift away from heavy industry and toward the service sector has been accompanied by the rise of labor-intensive manufacturing in new locations. More labor-intensive manufacturing, particularly assembly activities, is likely to be located in peripheral countries where labor is cheap, regulations (including environmental controls) are few, and tax rates are low. Elaborate trading networks and financial relations support the economic web at the heart of the new international division of labor. This new pattern has linked the world's economies more closely together, but it carries with it patterns of interaction that favor some areas over others.

Specialized Patterns

Developments discussed so far—the growing connections between the developed core and the newly industrialized countries, the decline of the older industrial areas, and the emergence of assembly-style manufacturing in the periphery—are not the only significant changes that have shaped the new global economic picture. One change that is altering the economic landscape of the contemporary world is the development of a set of links between *world cities*—major urban centers of multinational business and finance—the control centers of the world economy. These cities are not necessarily the largest in terms of population, nor are they the greatest centers of manufacturing. Instead, they are the places where the world's most important financial and corporate institutions are located and where decisions are made that divide the world economy. The basic pattern is shown in text Figure 27-3, which shows that most of the major world cities are located in the developed core. Thus a global economic geography dominated by nation-states is giving way to one in which world cities and multinational corporations play an increasingly significant role.

Time-Space Compression

A key theme of the last few decades is captured by the phrase *time-space compression*—a set of developments that have dramatically changed the way we think about time and space in the global economic arena. The rise of the World Wide Web plays into the time-space compression. It is too early to know what the full impact of the Web might be, but its role in reducing the importance of distance is self-evident. It also clearly plays a role in the decentralization of economic activity.

CHAPTER QUIZ

MULTIPLE-CHOICE QUESTIONS

1. The mass-production assembly line was pioneered by:
   a. J.P. Morgan
   b. Henry Ford
   c. Andrew Carnegie
   d. Henry Kaiser

2. Service industries are commonly referred to as:
   a. secondary industries
   b. tangible industries
   c. primary industries
   d. tertiary industries

3. One of the fastest-growing segments of the tourist industry is:
   a. golfing
   b. fishing
   c. cruising
   d. birding

4. In the early twenty-first century, five regions accounted for well over 75 percent of the world's total output of manufactured goods. Which of the following **is** one of these.
   a. western Russia and Ukraine
   b. southeastern Australia
   c. Eastern Europe
   d. South Asia

5. A number of so-called newly industrialized countries now have emerged as contributors to the global manufacturing base. Two are in the Americas and these are:
   a. Chile and Brazil
   b. Brazil and Mexico
   c. Argentina and Chile
   d. Mexico and Venezuela

6. Commercial production of television sets began after:
   a. the Korean War
   b. World War I
   c. World War II
   d. the Vietnam War

7. The American ideal of the university town originated in:
   a. Italy
   b. England
   c. France
   d. Germany

8. Maquiladora plants are an example of special economic zone development; these particular zones are located along the border between:
   a. the United States and Canada
   b. Mexico and the United States
   c. Spain and Portugal
   d. Italy and France

9. For many decades the Rühr Valley was associated with what kind of industry.
   a. iron and steel
   b. textiles
   c. footwear
   d. computers

10. Which continent has none of the World Cities that are becoming dominant in the global economy.
    a. South America
    b. Asia
    c. Africa
    d. Australia

TRUE/FALSE QUESTIONS

1. The mass-production assembly line did not affect any other industries except the making of cars. (TF)

2. Oil-extracting industries belong in the tertiary industry category. (TF)

3. One factor causing older industrial districts to decline is newer factories building elsewhere. (TF)

4. The process of deindustrialization did little to change the basic disparities between core and periphery. (TF)

5. Research and development activities are quaternary industries. (TF)

6. Labor-intensive manufacturing, particularly assembly activities, is more likely to be located in peripheral countries. (TF)

7. Many service industries do not need raw materials or use large amounts of energy. (TF)

8. World Cities are the largest in terms of population, and are the places where decisions are made that drive the world economy. (TF)

9. California's Silicon Valley is an example of a high-technology corridor. (TF)

10. The World Wide Web is playing a role in the decentralization of economic activity. (TF)

STUDY QUESTIONS

1. What event of the 1970s changed the role of core industrial regions? Discuss the service sector and its three categories. Discuss the largest service industry and its impact on countries.

2. Discuss the global shift in industrial production, including the tertiary sector—where and why. How and why has location changed in these industries? Discuss foreign investment and its role in location.

3. How do World Cities fit into the picture of today's global economy? Where are they located (text Figure 27-3)?

4. List and define the different kinds of specialized economic zones. Where are they located? Why have they been created?

5. What is meant by time-space compression? How has it affected the world? What is the World Wide Web and how has it already affected the world?

Notes

172

Notes

Notes

CHAPTER 28.   THE CHANGING NATURE OF THE CIVIC EXPERIENCE

CHAPTER INTRODUCTION

The urban influences affecting the modern cultural geography of today's world represent the end of a long evolutionary process resulting from the mixing of different cultures.

A city, regardless of the culture where it develops, represents society, culture, opportunity, success, and failure. Europe and America are urbanized societies whose cities and cultures are changing within an urban environment, a condition not true in the developing world. The cities and urban places of the developing world represent the greatest challenge to traditional cultures in the early twenty-first century. Developing societies face the formidable task of retaining their cultural identities and traditional values in a rapidly changing world. On their success or failure rests the successful existence of much of humanity.

Two centuries ago demographers estimate less than 5 percent of the world's population was urbanized. Today the figure approaches 50 percent and some regional differences and changes are striking, as in such countries as Germany and Belgium, where 90 percent of the population lives in cities and towns. In some parts of the world, megalopolises are evolving from formerly separate cities. In others, megacities are emerging with populations that exceed those of many countries. In this chapter we will discuss these regional changes and focus on several of the critical problems rapid urbanization has produced. As you will see, the problems of large cities are cross-cultural; they differ in degree, not in kind.

Urban America

The problems of urban America are especially severe in the *inner cities* and in the older *central business districts* (CBDs). While urban sprawl continues and cities are coalescing, people have left the inner cities by the millions and moved to the suburbs. The CBD is being reduced to serving the inner-most portion of the metropolis. As manufacturing employment in the core are has declined, many large cities have adapted by promoting a shift toward service industries. Beyond the CBDs of many large cities, however, the vast inner cities remain problem-ridden domains of low- and moderate-income people, most of whom live there because they have nowhere else to go.

In older industrial cities, the inner city has become a landscape of inadequate housing, sub-standard living, and widespread decay. Many of the buildings are now worn out, unsanitary, and infested by rats and cockroaches. Apartments are overfilled with people who cannot escape the vicious cycle that forces them to live there.

The Suburban City

For many decades the attraction of country life with city amenities, reinforced by the discomforts of living in the heart of many central cities, has propelled people to move to the suburbs and more distant urban fringes. Mass commuting from suburban residences to downtown workplaces was made possible in post–WW II times by the automobile. As a result, the kind of suburbanization that is familiar to North Americans and other Westerners became a characteristic of urbanization in mobile, highly developed societies.

Today's suburban cities are not just self-sufficient, but compete with the central city for leading urban economic activities such as telecommunications, high-technology industries, and corporate headquarters. In the current era of *globalization*, America's suburban cities are proving their power to attract such activities, thereby sustaining the suburbanizing process. Suburbanization has expanded the American city far into the surrounding countryside, contributing to the impoverishment of the central cities, and is having a major impact on community life.

The European City

European cities are older than North American cities, but they too were transformed by the Industrial Revolution. Indeed, industrialization struck many of Europe's dormant medieval towns and vibrant mercantile cities like a landslide. But there are differences between the European experience and that of North America.

In terms of population numbers, the great European cities are in the same class as major North American cities. London, Paris, Madrid, and Berlin are megacities by world standards. These are among Europe's historic urban centers, which have been affected but not engulfed by the industrial tide. The cities of the British Midlands and the megacities of Germany's Ruhr are more representative of the manufacturing era.

The industrial cities have lost much of their historical heritage, but in Europe's largest cities the legacy of the past is better preserved. Many European cities have a *Greenbelt*—a zone of open country averaging up to 20 miles wide that contains scattered small towns but is otherwise open country. This has the effect of containing the built-up area and preserving near-urban open space. For this reason, European cities have not yet experienced the dispersal of their U.S. counterparts, and remain more compact and clustered. Modern CBDs have emerged near the historic cores of these cities.

CHAPTER QUIZ

MULTIPLE-CHOICE QUESTIONS

1. In the 1980s and 1990s, political developments on the western Pacific Rim had an impact on Canada. The principal city affected was:
   a. Regina
   b. Vancouver
   c. Montreal
   d. Edmonton

2. When migrants seek asylum, documentation may not be available and claims cannot be easily checked and these people must be confined to special facilities. This has become a contentious political issue in Europe, especially in:
   a. France
   b. Germany
   c. the United Kingdom
   d. Spain

3. In American cities, the so-called inner cities are located:
   a. in the center of the new suburbs
   b. in the center of the old CBD
   c. between the new suburbs
   d. between the CBD and the suburbs

4. This development has devastated the commercial core of many a modest-sized American city:
   a. suburban shopping malls
   b. lack of adequate parking for shoppers
   c. loss of public transportation
   d. influx of entertainment establishments

5. Large Canadian cities:
   a. suffer from a lack of good planning
   b. are spread out
   c. have a better tax base and offer better services
   d. have slums larger than American cities

6. In many of Europe's largest dominant cities:
   a. wars have wiped out the manufacturing areas
   b. the past is better preserved
   c. suburban areas compete with the central city
   d. government planning has had 300 years to develop

7. Which of the following is **not** a characteristic of communist planned cities.
   a. wide streets with little traffic
   b. microdistricts
   c. ugly apartment blocks
   d. a vital central business district

8. In many inner cities in America the outflow of the urban population has been reversed by:
   a. gentrification
   b. free public transportation
   c. urban "homesteading"
   d. lower taxes

9. In the post–WW II era, which of the following made suburbanization of the type familiar to North Americans and other Westerners a characteristic of urbanization in mobile, highly developed societies.
   a. improved public transportation
   b. cleaner air standards
   c. the automobile
   d. gentrification

10 The essence of the modern American city is the:
   a. revitalized CBD
   b. suburbs
   c. central cities
   d. surrounding rural areas

TRUE/FALSE QUESTIONS

1. European cities do not have durable ethnic neighborhoods. (TF)

2. Today, Mexico City houses between one-fifth and one-quarter of the country's entire population. (TF)

3. In today's world, the money that emigrants to a Western country send back home makes a critical difference in the poorer countries of the world. (TF)

4. Many older downtowns in America today are reaping the benefits of agglomeration. (TF)

5. Many areas once called suburbs have become cities in their own right. (TF)

6. Canada's large cities are more compact and still have large numbers of high- and middle-income people living in the central city. (TF)

7. Many European cities have greenbelts surrounding the central city. (TF)

8. Communist planners attempted to create microdistricts in cities. This led to many cities not having a central downtown district. (TF)

9. Canada's largest city is Vancouver. (TF)

10 Western European cities tend to be far less compact than Canadian or American cities. (TF)

STUDY QUESTIONS

1. List the problems in America's central (CBD) cities. Why do these problems exist? What efforts are being made to reverse this trend? How have the original suburbs evolved?

2. How do European cities differ from American cities? What are some of the factors that have made European cities different?

3. By the middle of the twenty-first century, as much as 75 percent of the world's population may be concentrated in cities and towns. Some scholars argue that over the long term, this will be a positive change, while others are predicting a detrimental impact to the planet. List the major arguments in support of this change, and the major concerns against. Which group do you think is right?

Notes

Notes

CHAPTER 29.   CULTURE CHANGE IN AN ERA OF GLOBALIZATION

CHAPTER INTRODUCTION

Some 500 years ago, at the beginning of the era of Exploration and Discovery, major cultures existed in the world with a minimum of contact with each other, some more isolated than others. One of these cultures, the European, spread farther and faster than others and had a greater impact through of the process of colonialism. The impact of the global diffusion of the European culture did much to shape the world as we know it today.

While it is true that cultures have affected one another through history, even before European colonization, the extent and scale of interaction has greatly increased over the past century. Spurred on by greater human mobility and advances in technology, the globalization of culture has eroded the distinction between folk culture and popular culture, which fosters the development of new identity communities that cut across traditional cultural lines.

Economic and cultural globalization are closely linked, and that link has led cultural products increasingly to be seen as commodities to be bought and sold. The twin impacts of economic and cultural globalization make it increasingly important to see individual places in relation to other places and to processes unfolding at extralocal scales. The distinctiveness of individual places is threatened, often resulting in efforts to protect endogenous products.

A fundamental point is that cultural change in an era of globalization is about the ways that a variety of place-specific cultural ideas and practices shape globalization and are, in turn, shaped by it. Place-based cultural ideas and practices are deeply implicated both in the creation of a certain type of globalization and in the impacts of that globalization on particular people and places.

Changing Cultural Interaction

Virtually all places experience cultural interaction, but the extent and scale of interaction has not been uniform across time or space, and in some cases it has produced far greater changes in a short time than in others. Historically, change has tended to be the greatest in the face of rapid developments in the technology of communication or warfare, but rapid change has also occurred when a society brings new diseases into an area where the inhabitants lack resistance to those diseases. Thus colonialism was far more than a political and economic affair.

Folk cultures are a fading phenomenon in the industrialized cultures of the world and are disappearing in the global periphery as well. The scope and speed of globalization today raises questions about how meaningful it is to try and distinguish between folk and popular cultures, since any folk culture has been affected in some significant way by so-called popular cultures.

At the heart of the blurring of folk and popular culture are the extraordinary changes over the past 100 years in the time it takes for people, innovations, and ideas to spread around the globe. During the past century, the pace of diffusion has shrunk from decades and years to months, weeks, days, and even hours.

Finally, we must remember that there are significant geographical differences in the access people have to the things that facilitate the movement of cultural products, ideas, and people. As a result, some peoples and places are able to exert a much greater external influence than are others, even though that influence and exposure does not always lead to acceptance.

Impacts of Cultural Globalization

One of the most obvious consequences of cultural globalization is the increasing dominance around the world of particular cultural forms produced in specific places. The point here is that the cultural forms produced in a relatively few places exert an influence greatly disproportionate to their size, and while cultures around the world are not all becoming alike, cultural diversity can suffer when a narrow range of cultural forms exerts an extraordinary degree of dominance.

Among the most far-reaching consequences of the link between economic and cultural globalization is the tendency for a growing number of things to be thought of, and treated as, commodities to be exchanged for money—a process termed *commodification*. Many societies had no tradition of treating new ideas as something to be bought and sold, and the development of an increasingly globalized market-based economy reaching into all parts of the globe has important economic, social, *and* cultural consequences.

While it is clear that the impacts of globalization on culture change are many and far reaching, one point is important to reiterate. The homogenizing impacts of globalization are highly variable, and even where the impacts are the greatest, one cannot speak of cultural convergence in any meaningful sense. The same cultural form or process will not have the same impact in different places because the culture of these places differs to begin with.

Reactions to Cultural Globalization

Cultural globalization is both rejected and embraced. From a geographical perspective, the important point is that the range of reactions—often working together in the same place—is shaping the character of places and landscapes. At the heart of the reaction to cultural globalization is the concern that acceptance of external ideas and innovations will result in the loss of local distinctiveness and identity.

It is the very appeal of external cultural forms that promotes concerns about their implications for local distinctiveness and identity. Human beings define themselves in significant part by the communities and places to which they feel a sense of attachment or belonging. They often vehemently resist any threat to these feelings. There are, however, few instances where such resistance has been truly successful.

CHAPTER QUIZ

MULTIPLE-CHOICE QUESTIONS

1. In the 1990s, it was said that more people around the world knew who this man was than any other individual.
   a. Bill Clinton
   b. Michael Jordan
   c. Bill Gates
   d. Sammy Sosa

2. Three hundred years ago, in a small fishing village along the Norwegian coast, one of the symbols of exterior cultural influence would have been a/an __?__ church.
   a. Catholic
   b. Episcopal
   c. Lutheran
   d. Methodist

3. The stage was set for the remarkable decline in the distance decay of innovation diffusion by:
   a. the Internet
   b. air travel
   c. television
   d. European colonization

4. At the global scale, which of the following is **not** presently one of the three areas of greatest global cultural influence.
   a. South Asia
   b. North America
   c. East Asia
   d. western Europe

5. The so-called Reality TV phenomenon in the United States today has its roots in:
   a. Germany and France
   b. the United Kingdom and Sweden
   c. Australia
   d. Japan

6. Which of the following countries currently provides heavy subsidies to its domestic film industry to help encourage and promote local cultural productions.
   a. Canada
   b. Germany
   c. Australia
   d. France

7. In the last few years, the once distinctly North American way of celebrating Halloween has diffused to various parts of the world—particularly to:
   a. Eastern Europe
   b. China
   c. western Europe
   d. Japan

8. Which of the following is an extreme example of the growing tendency to transpose landscape ideals from one place to another.
   a. the strip in Las Vegas, Nevada
   b. Disneyland in Anaheim, California
   c. Sea World in Orlando, Florida
   d. Coney Island in New York City, New York

9. In which of the following countries did the ruling regime pursue isolationist policies in the late 1990s and early twenty-first century.
   a. India
   b. Afghanistan
   c. Indonesia
   d. Pakistan

10. The term *syncretism*, meaning that elements from different cultural sources are combined in novel ways to create something new, was originally developed in:
   a. psychology
   b. sociology
   c. political science
   d. anthropology

TRUE/FALSE QUESTIONS

1. Economic and cultural globalization are closely linked. (TF) T

2. The country of Nepal now relies on tourist spending for one-half of its foreign earnings. (TF) T

3. Virtually all cultures at all times have been the product of cultural interactions among diverse peoples. (TF) T

4. Colonialism was far more than a political and economic affair. (TF) T

5. The most concrete expression of the homogenizing tendency of cultural globalization is not usually found in the cultural landscape. (TF) F

6. Today, there are still significant geographical differences in the access people have to the things that facilitate the movement of cultural products, ideas, and people. (TF) T

7. Although the impacts of globalization on culture are many and far reaching, the homogenizing impacts are highly variable and true cultural convergence does not actually occur. (TF) T

8. The notion of global local continuum emphasizes that what happens at one scale is independent of what happens at another. (TF) T

9. In Belgium, Austria, and Italy, substantial numbers of voters are favoring candidates for election with strong anti-immigration views. (TF) F

10. Various forms of resistance to the globalization of culture are widespread and there are numerous instances where these efforts have been completely successful. (TF) F

STUDY QUESTIONS

1. Using the material in your text, define globalization in your own words. List some examples of both cultural and economic diffusion that have affected this process.

2. How has globalization affected and changed the cultural landscape of some of the world's cultural regions? List some specific examples. What were the sources of these changes?

3. Despite some instances of strong resistance to local cultural changes by external influences, total success is virtually impossible. List some reasons such resistance is rarely successful.

Notes

Notes

PART TEN: SOCIAL GEOGRAPHIES OF THE MODERN WORLD

CHAPTER 30. GLOBAL DISPARITIES IN NUTRITION AND HEALTH

CHAPTER INTRODUCTION

Humans must have food to survive. Hunting and gathering provided a precarious existence, but with the development of agriculture, surpluses of food could be produced. Concerns about food supplies and population appear periodically but predicted global shortages have not materialized. Yet there is hunger, even in an affluent country like the United States. The portion of this chapter that examines the geography of nutrition should cause you to consider not the success of the past, but the question of a hungry world of the future.

Just twenty years ago, predictions of regional famines in countries with large populations and high growth rates regularly made headlines, and the warnings seemed to have a sound basis: population growth was outpacing the Earth's capacity to provide enough food, let alone distribute it where it was most needed. Today, daily caloric consumption still varies from high levels in the richer countries such as the United States, Canada, European states, Japan, and Australia to very low levels in poorer countries of Africa. Yet the overall situation has markedly improved over conditions two decades ago.

Distribution of Dietary Patterns

The map of average daily calorie consumption (text Figure 30-1) is based on data that are not always reliable, so it gives only a general impression of the global situation. Statistical information about caloric intake, especially for countries in the periphery, is often based on rough estimates rather than on accurate counts. Nevertheless, the map rather clearly reveals the world distribution of hunger and *malnutrition*—conditions of ill health resulting from the deficiency or improper balance of essential foodstuffs in the diet. Compare text Figure 30-1 to the map of world population distribution in text Figure 4-1 and it will be apparent that malnutrition still afflicts and shortens the lives of hundreds of millions of people, especially children, who are often the first victims in villages when food supplies dwindle. It is also worth mentioning that the scale of text Figure 30-1 precludes identifying pockets of malnutrition, which occur even within many of the better-nourished countries where pockets of poverty still exist.

The Distribution of Health

Americans take good health for granted. It may be expensive, but the capacity for good health is present in our society, as it is in all developed countries. For much of the world's population, especially those residing in tropical areas and other poorer countries, the situation is quite different. Good health, like adequate food, is unevenly distributed. Patterns of health show even greater regional differences than those for the distribution of food. When people are inadequately fed they are susceptible to many debilitating diseases. Similarly, women who are healthy tend to bear healthy babies, but women who suffer from malnutrition and related maladies are less fortunate. In many poorer countries people, especially children, are visibly malnourished. The resulting disadvantages will be with them for life—if they survive childhood.

The study of health in geographic context is called *medical geography*. Many diseases have their origin in the environment. They have source (core) areas, spread (diffuse) through populations along identifiable routes, and affect clusters of populations (regions) when at their widest distribution. Mapping disease patterns can provide insights into relationships between diseases and environment and sometimes give clues to source regions.

Malnutrition and Child Mortality

It is difficult to identify the specific effects of malnutrition on people's susceptibility to disease because so many other factors are present. However, there is little doubt about the effects of malnutrition on growth and development. The impact on children is especially important, because they are often the first to be affected when food supplies become inadequate.

Infant and child mortality reflect the overall health of a society. *Infant mortality* is recorded as a baby's death during the first year following its birth; *child mortality* records death between ages 1 and 5. The map showing the world distribution of infant mortality (text Figure 30-1) reveals the high rates in many poorer countries. The map also clearly shows the relationship between social disorder and high infant mortality rates (IMRs). Conflict, dislocation, and refugee movements produce high IMRs, and the map reflects this.

Even if there is general adequacy of available calories, *protein deficiencies* still have a devastating affect on children, as they do for entire populations. In tropical areas especially, dietary deficiencies inhibit the development of young bodies, and the resultant problems follow children through their entire lives.

Types and Patterns of Disease

The incidence and types of diseases that affect a population, like life expectancy, also reveal the conditions in which people live. Certain kinds of environments harbor dangerous disease carriers, and diseases have ways of spreading from one population to another. Medical geographers are interested in both the regional distribution of diseases and the processes and paths whereby diseases spread or diffuse.

Tropical areas, wherein are located many of the world's people (see text Figures 3-5 and 4-1), are zones of intense biological activity and hence are the sources of many disease-transmitting viruses and parasites. Certain major diseases remain contained within tropical or near-tropical latitudes (much of this is due to limited environment tolerance by these diseases), but others have spread into all parts of the world. Before European exploration and colonization, many diseases were limited to regional outbreaks (called *epidemics*) and took on global significance only when they were carried to all parts of the globe (termed *pandemics*). As transportation improved and human movement on a global scale increased, so did the spread of many diseases. AIDS, for example, originated in tropical Africa and is now a global pandemic.

In the rapidly expanding urban areas of periphery countries today, densely populated shantytowns with inadequate sanitation and contaminated water supplies are highly susceptible to out-breaks of disease. In December 1990, a cholera outbreak began in the slums of Lima, Peru and by early 1995 had killed more than 10,000 people with more than a million cases reported in every country in the Western Hemisphere. And cholera is a disease whose causes are known and prevention and treatment are possible.

Dramatic as are the global pandemics of AIDS, influenza, or cholera, the number of cases of heart disease, cancer, stroke, and lung ailments are far greater. These *chronic diseases* (also known as degenerative diseases and generally associated with old age) have always been the leading causes of death and remain so today in the United States (see Table 30-2) and throughout the

Western world. Problems of chronic diseases are as heavily concentrated in the urban, industrial core as are some of the major infectious diseases that prevail in the periphery (text Figure 30-14).

CHAPTER QUIZ

MULTIPLE-CHOICE QUESTIONS

1. Which of the following is most vital to a child in the first three years of life.
   a. carbohydrates
   b. proteins
   c. fats
   d. minerals

2. Which of the following continents has benefitted the least from the Green Revolution.
   a. Asia
   b. South America
   c. Europe
   d. Africa

3. With few exceptions, the countries where caloric intake is low are also those where __?__ are in short supply.
   a. carbohydrates
   b. fats
   c. proteins
   d. minerals

4. Text Figure 30-1 shows that the comparatively rich countries are also the best-fed, and that __?__ is currently in the worst position.
   a. Sub-Saharan Africa
   b. Southwest Asia
   c. Eastern Europe
   d. South America

5. The consumption of __?__ by people in wealthier countries puts an enormous strain on economies and ecologies elsewhere.
   a. tropical fruit
   b. meat
   c. coffee
   d. vegetables

6. The lowest infant mortality rate among larger populations has long been reported by:
   a. the United States
   b. Sweden
   c. Japan
   d. France

7. Chronic diseases are the diseases of:
   a. longevity
   b. youth
   c. males only
   d. females only

8. In Peru in 1990, there was an outbreak of which of the following diseases that killed 10,000 people.
   a. influenza
   b. cholera
   c. yellow fever
   d. malaria

9. Influenza originally came from:
   a. China
   b. India
   c. Brazil
   d. South Africa

10. Which two continents suffer the most from yellow fever.
    a. Asia and Africa
    b. Australia and Africa
    c. Africa and South America
    d. Asia and Europe

TRUE/FALSE QUESTIONS

1. One of the main reasons people do not have adequate food in poorer countries is the lack of good transportation. (TF)

2. Adult males in poorer countries suffer more from malnutrition than children because they cannot work. (TF)

3. There are nine key areas that can be addressed to help prevent another world food crisis. (TF)

4. Despite the fact that the specter of global famine is receding from newspaper headlines, a major perturbation in global climate could reverse the favorable trends of the past 25 years. (TF)

5. Medical geographers can map diseases as they diffuse from their core area. (TF)

6. Poor sanitation is the key factor in high infant mortality rates. (TF)

7. Average life expectancy may vary from rich to poor countries, but in all cases women outlive men. (TF)

8. When a disease spreads around the world it is called an epidemic. (TF)

9. Malaria, yellow fever, sleeping sickness, and bilbarzia are vectored diseases caused by mosquitos or flies. (TF)

10. There were over 28 million cases of AIDS in Africa in 2002. (TF)

STUDY QUESTIONS

1. Looking at text Figure 30-1, which continent has the worst-fed countries? List the problems encountered by these countries that contribute to their food shortages.

2. How are infant and child mortality defined in the text? What are the causes of kwashiorkor and marasmus?

3. What are the main factors that contribute to infant mortality? Looking at text Figure 30-1, which countries are shown in the highest category of infant mortality? Discuss infant mortality in the different world regions and variations within each region.

4. What are the three major types of disease? Discuss the major vectored diseases: what is the vector, how do they spread, are they worldwide, how do they affect people? Use the figures in your text to help you find the core areas of these different diseases.

5. How are nonvectored infectious diseases spread? Which of these has reached the pandemic stage many times? Using text Figure 30-11 and accompanying text material, explain how the cause of this disease was discovered. Discuss the spread of AIDS. Where are infection rates the highest?

Notes

Notes

Notes

CHAPTER 31.   GEOGRAPHIES OF INEQUALITY: RACE AND ETHNICITY

CHAPTER INTRODUCTION

All humans belong to the *human race*. For a variety of reasons human groups do differ physically from one another (there are physical differences *within* the human race, not *between* races) and, unfortunately, it is these differences that have become synonymous with the word "race." Many societies have used these differences to create distinctions in status and opportunity among individuals.

Ours is a world of inequalities—of unequal opportunities, advantages, privileges. The disparities apply across the board, to entire countries, to majorities and minorities within those countries, and to individuals in those societies. Dominant majorities in multicultural states create and sustain systems designed to protect their privileges. Members of minority groups find their upward path blocked by racial or ethnic discrimination. Women the world over suffer from mistreatment in male-dominated societies.

This chapter should be studied carefully, for with the many problems facing humanity in the twenty-first century, racial conflict is an unneeded burden, and there is no doubt about the biological unity of the human species. We also need to keep in mind that what is often called "racial" conflict is nothing of the sort. Take the case of the recent disastrous breakdown of order in Rwanda. The Western press implied a genuine difference exists between the Tutsi and the Hutu "races." In fact, no one can discern a Tutsi from a Hutu just by physical appearance. The war was over status, advantage, and opportunity. The conflict was cultural or ethnic, not "racial." Yet hundreds of thousands died.

A Geography of Race

Humans may think that they look quite different but it is not appearance that is the key. Rather, it is the *genetic* makeup of the individuals. Within a species, the chromosomes of reproducing organisms are identical in number and size, and they carry very similar groups of *genes*. Groups of individuals *within* a species display certain physical characteristics that tend to set them apart from others. In the human species, these groups (sometimes called *subspecies* or *populations*) exhibit regional variation. This results *not* from differences in the fundamental genetic makeup of each group but from differences in *gene frequency* among populations.

So human populations vary and their differences are, in part, matters of physical appearance. What is often called race is in fact a combination of physical attributes in a population, the product of a particular genetic inheritance that dominates in that population (such as Australia's Aborigines, North Africa's Berbers, or Asia's Mongols). This inheritance varies from one population to another, and probably results from a long history of adaptation to different environments. For this reason, the use of the term race for such populations is in error.

Race as a Social Category

Many societies around the world treat race as significant and a large number of people believe that those of different races—however defined—are in some way inferior. *Racism* is, therefore, part of the human condition, and it has both geographic expression and geographic consequences. When guestworkers are attacked in a country, it is the product of a flow of people from one part of the world to another. Such attacks are concentrated in areas where social problems are more acute and nationalism has taken root among the young. In these and many other instances, racism influences the organization of people and places in ways that have significant impacts on possibilities and opportunities.

Racism is often associated with a degree of segregation that promotes stereotypes and influences where people go and what they do. Race is a particularly notable feature of the internal geography of many American urban areas, and some large cities are remarkably segregated along urban lines. But the significance of segregation goes beyond who lives where; it can promote stereotypes of racial neighborhoods and foster arrangements and perceptions that affect what people do and where they do it. Understanding racial patterns at various scales can reveal important aspects of the way human beings create communities and relate to one another.

Ethnicity

Ethnicity defies easy definition or description (*ethnic* is defined as a combination of a people's culture [traditions, customs, language, and religion] and racial ancestry), but in actual practice its defining characteristics differ from place to place. A map showing all recognizable ethnic areas might be no larger than a neighborhood or as large as an entire country.

But size is no measure of the intensity of ethnic pride and solidarity. Such feelings are deepened by shared cultural traits, a common history, a treasured cultural landscape, or a real or potential threat to language or faith. So-called "racial" ancestry may or may not play a part in this, and ethnicity should not be equated with race-consciousness. Ethnic conflict intensifies when hostile groups perceive themselves to be of different ancestry, but it is culture, not race that dominates in shaping the world's ethnic patterns and processes. Ethnicity is of very real significance in the contemporary world.

Ethnic Conflict

Territory is at the root of ethnic conflict. The global political order is organized around nation-states whose governments theoretically control the territory of the state in the name of the nation. But the concept of the nation itself is often tied to a particular sense of ethnic identity, which in turn can lead members of different ethnic groups to resist the control of national governments. This is particularly true when ethnic groups living in political territories that are defined and governed by the national ambitions of other ethnic groups face frustration because of a real or perceived slighting by the central government.

CHAPTER QUIZ

MULTIPLE-CHOICE QUESTIONS

1. The idea that skin color is a particularly important way of dividing humans is rooted in:
    a. biology
    b. culture
    c. environment
    d. geographic location

2. What is often called a race is in fact a combination of __?__ attributes in a population.
    a. cultural
    b. ethnic
    c. economic
    d. physical

3. Skin color is a matter of pigmentation. This pigment is called:
   a. DNA
   b. epithelial
   c. melanin
   d. caratin

4. The highest intensity of skin pigmentation is found in the:
   a. tropics and subtropics
   b. middle and high latitudes
   c. subtropics and high latitudes
   d. tropics and middle latitudes

5. The U. S. Civil Rights Act was passed in:
   a. 1984
   b. 1974
   c. 1954
   d. 1964

6. The term *ethnic* comes from the ancient Greek word *ethnos,* meaning:
   a. state
   b. people or nation
   c. race
   d. culture

7. Which of the following urban areas has an ethnic neighborhood called Little Havana.
   a. Houston
   b. Atlanta
   c. Miami
   d. New Orleans

8. The root of most ethnic conflict is:
   a. territory
   b. economics
   c. food shortages
   d. skin color

9. In 1763, what would become Canada was ceded to Britain by:
   a. the United States
   b. Spain
   c. Portugal
   d. France

10. The largest Canadian province is:
    a. Prince Edward Island
    b. Quebec
    c. Alberta
    d. Ontario

TRUE/FALSE QUESTIONS

1. The term race focuses on differences rather than on similarities. (TF)

2. The different outward appearance of humans can be attributed gene frequency. (TF)

3. People with dark skin have less melanin pigment than those with light skin. (TF)

4. Conflicts between groups are actually cultural, not racial. (TF)

5. Because of the interaction between different ethnic groups in today's world, ethnicity is not the issue it used to be. (TF)

6. When many ethnic groups came to America, they tried to settle in places that resembled their home country. (TF)

7. Race is no longer a notable feature of the internal geography of many American urban areas. (TF)

8. The Quebec Parliament passed a law compelling all businesses to demonstrate they can function in French. (TF)

9. The first thing people notice about another person is the shape of their nose. (TF)

10. Jews and Palestinians are easily identified as being different because of skin color. (TF)

STUDY QUESTIONS

1. Discuss the use of the word race. When differences are noted in a person's physical appearance, what are you actually seeing? Discuss the various physical traits that make people appear different.

2. How is the term ethnic used? How does ethnicity fit with culture? Briefly describe the situation in former Yugoslavia with regard to race, ethnicity, culture, and religion. How does acculturation affect ethnic identity?

3. Briefly, using the major points in your text, describe the history and current situation in Quebec, Canada.

Notes

Notes

CHAPTER 32.   GENDER INEQUALITIES IN GEOGRAPHIC PERSPECTIVE

CHAPTER INTRODUCTION

Women slightly outnumber men in the world. In other words, numerically, men and women are almost equal. The "equality" stops there, however. In virtually every country of the world the position and status of women is less than men. We have already seen that ours is a world of racial diversity, cultural variety, and economic disparity. The inequality between men and women is another kind of inequality—inequality between the sexes, sometimes referred to by the term *gender*, a term that connotes social situation, not just biology. The plight of women is undefendable in much of the world and is a subject that demands our attention.

A Geography of Gender
When topics such as population growth, migration, or food production arise, they tend to be discussed in the aggregate. When a country's high population growth rate is cited as a possible threat to its future stability or its development potential, we may not consider the situation of the women who bear the children, and raise them, then are confined to a village—possibly for life. Men suffer no such constraints, and men and women born and raised in the same village live in completely different worlds.

Demographic statistics for individual countries (or divisions within countries) tend to conceal gender gaps—differences between females and males ranging from life expectancy to literacy rates. Often this is deliberate on the part of a government, but it may also be due simply to conditions within the country. In poorer countries the majority of the population may be rural dwellers, and in contrast to wealthy, developed countries, little attention is paid to rural areas. Since taking an accurate census is difficult and expensive, it is not a high priority of many governments. When you add to this the perceived lower status of women in many traditional societies, accurate information becomes impossible.

Modernization and economic development reduce inequalities between men and women, but they do not eliminate them. In Western Europe, the United States, and Japan equality has not been achieved. Large wage differences remain, and barriers to social and economic advancement persist. In corporate, political, and many other settings, maps of inequality can still be drawn. Despite the persistence of gender inequality, however, women in urban, industrial societies made enormous progress during the twentieth century, in stark contrast to what occurred in more traditional societies.

Life Expectancy
In most of the world's countries, women outlive men for periods ranging from less than one year to ten years or more—termed the *longevity gap*. Population pyramids show that for certain countries women outnumber men, especially in the higher age categories. The average gender-longevity gap is about four years, but this differential varies spatially (text Figure 32-1). In countries where life is especially difficult for women the closing of the longevity gap reflects this.

Figures on life-expectancy say nothing about quality of life. During their lifetimes, women's health problems and concerns differ from those of men. According to a UN study, pregnant women in the poorer realms face health risks 80 to 600 times greater than those faced by women in the richer countries (text Figure 32-2). South Asian women suffer the highest *maternal mortality,* but the risk for African women is nearly as high. Inadequate medical services, an excessive number of pregnancies, and malnutrition are among the leading causes of maternal death in poorer countries.

Population-Control Policies

Women may live longer than men, and in the upper age categories women may outnumber men, but in early life it is another story. Female infanticide and the abortion of female fetuses (aborted after gender detection tests) occur widely in India, China, and other countries where tradition and economics combine to threaten girls and women. Many thousands of female infants are killed each year according to a UNICEF report, but the modern techniques of prenatal gender detection contribute far more to the imbalance between male and female.

Both India and China have a traditional preference for male offspring, and both countries are experiencing an imbalance between men and women as a result of the practices described above. In 1994, the UN reported that India as a whole had 133 single men for every 100 single women and some Indian states report wider differences. But there is an important difference between the problems in China and India. In India, female infanticide appears to be most prevalent in remote rural areas and the same is true in China. But the one-child policy introduced by the Chinese government in the past was most effective in urban and near-urban areas. Thus female infanticide increased substantially in China's more-developed areas, where the scarcity of female marriage partners has now become acute.

Economy and Production

Work performed by women as unpaid labor in households and on the land would, if measured in monetary value, increase the world's total paid production by about one-third. In the poorer countries women produce more than half the food (70 percent in Africa), transport water and firewood, build dwellings, and perform numerous other tasks. From a purely practical point of view, ignoring the economic contribution of women in a culture (or denying them the opportunity) makes poor fiscal sense.

Despite these conditions, the number of women in the "official" workforce is rising. All but one geographic realm showed increases between 1970 and 1990 (in Sub-Saharan Africa, the percentage of women in the labor force actually declined). It is sad but true that women continue to be the last to benefit from job expansion and the first to suffer from job contraction—particularly in the stagnant or declining economies of Africa, Latin America, and the Caribbean.

CHAPTER QUIZ

MULTIPLE-CHOICE QUESTIONS

1. In most of __?__ and all of Africa, the great majority of wage-earning women still work in agriculture.
   a. South America
   b. Asia
   c. Eastern Europe
   d. Oceania

2. In this region of the world women suffer the highest maternal mortality rate.
   a. East Asia
   b. Africa
   c. South America
   d. South Asia

3. During their reproductive years, women need nearly __?__ times as much iron in their diet as men.
   a. four
   b. five
   c. three
   d. six

4. In __?__ over 70 percent of girls are married by age 15.
   a. Mauritania
   b. Bangladesh
   c. Turkey
   d. Japan

5. In this country, the victorious Islamic Taliban movement in 1997 resulted in severely restricted rights for women.
   a. Afghanistan
   b. Iraq
   c. Pakistan
   d. Sudan

6. Equal educational opportunities are still lagging for girls in:
   a. South and East Asia
   b. Sub-Saharan Africa and South America
   c. North Africa and South Asia
   d. Sub-Saharan Africa and South Asia

7. In Africa south of the Sahara, it is estimated that women produce __?__ percent of the food.
   a. 100
   b. 70
   c. 80
   d. 90

8. Which continent has the highest women's education as a ratio to men's.
   a. South America
   b. Europe
   c. North America
   d. Asia

9. Between 1970 and 1990, women in the labor force increased in all but which geographic realm.
   a. Southwest Asia
   b. East Asia
   c. Sub-Saharan Africa
   d. South Asia

10. The first country to grant women the right to vote was New Zealand. The second was:
    a. Australia
    b. the United States
    c. Switzerland
    d. Sweden

TRUE-FALSE QUESTIONS

1. Modernization and economic development have given women equal status in society. (TF)

2. India has laws against female infanticide and dowry payments, but they are not enforced. (TF)

3. Islamic women are now allowed to wear modern dress in public as well as in the privacy of their own homes. (TF)

4. In India's southern State of Kerala, women are better educated, enjoy better health, and have fewer children. (TF)

5. In Middle and South America, illiteracy rates are highest in urban areas because most people migrating from rural areas are not able to afford to send children to school. (TF)

6. Women produce more than half the food in periphery countries. (TF)

7. Women in Africa can gain title to land when they are the head of a household. (TF)

8. Quality of life is lowest for women in South Asia. (TF)

9. Many women in poorer countries engage in "informal" activities to advance above the subsistence level. (TF)

10. Switzerland did not give women the right to vote until 1971. (TF)

STUDY QUESTIONS

1. Despite the fact that women tend to live longer in most of the world's countries, what factors affect their quality of life? Looking at text Figure 32-2, which countries have the highest maternal mortality?

2. According to your text, what two countries practice female infanticide and female fetus abortion? Is this legal in both countries? What are the effects of these practices? How do these countries differ in where these practices occur?

3. Discuss the treatment of women in India and in all Muslim countries. How do they differ?

4. Have women achieved total equality in the wealthier developed regions of the world? How do women fare in the political scene? How is this beginning to change?

Notes

Notes

PART ELEVEN: THE CHANGING ENVIRONMENTAL CONTEXT

CHAPTER 33. THE PLANET AND HUMANITY

CHAPTER INTRODUCTION

The Earth is incredibly old when compared to the way that humans think about age. A person reaching the age of 100 is still newsworthy even today, and at the end of the transition from the twentieth to the twenty-first century it was not uncommon to read about someone born in 1899 and still alive in 2001! This meant that they had lived in parts of three different centuries and two different millennia. Yet this is such a short period in Earth's history that it cannot be easily measured in geologic time—the way that the age of the Earth is measured (see text Figure 33-1).

Your text offers an interesting comparison of geologic time with what we will call "human" time. A "human" age of 100+ may mean a person can give an eyewitness account of the transition from horse-and-wagon to the automobile; the invention of the airplane and space travel; and the telegraph, telephone, and World Wide Web; but the rather brief temporal experience represents a minuscule portion of Earth history.

Assume that you are about 20 years of age with the known age of the Earth at 4.6 billion years. Each of your years is equal to 240 million Earth years, and one week a little less than 5 million years. One day corresponds to 700,000 years, and one hour, approximately 30,000 years.

By comparison, *Homo sapiens* appeared less than six hours ago, and modern human civilization, from the development of agriculture to suburbanization, has occupied the last twenty minutes. The Industrial Revolution is less than 30 seconds old, and accurate instrumental measurement of weather conditions has been going on for 17 seconds.

This raises a very valid question. How representative is the short-term present of the long-term past? During the twentieth century, geographers and other scientists embarked on a joint mission to reconstruct our planet's history on the basis of current evidence. Climatologist-geographer Alfred Wegener was one of the first to contribute to this venture with his hypothesis of continental drift, and many other theories and hypotheses from other scientists followed.

Part Eleven touches on some complex subjects that are only beginning to be understood: the history of environmental change on Planet Earth, the current environmental picture, and the relationships between human society and activity and natural environments. Environmental change is a hallmark of Planet Earth, and understanding long-term change helps us to cope with the present and prepare for the future. Since Earth's very early history, environmental change on a global scale has been caused by natural events some of which were catastrophic and calamitous. Even though *Homo sapiens* has caused changes in the environment, humans have not been dominant long enough to really have experience with Earth's early types of natural, planet-wide events.

Ocean and Atmosphere

Planet Earth today is often called the "Blue Planet" because more than 70 percent of its surface is covered by water and views from space are dominated by blue hues and swirls of white cloud, but in truth we do not know with any certainty how or when Earth acquired its watery cloak. Several hypotheses have been developed but none offer a complete answer or are universally accepted.

One reason for the concern is that our neighboring planet Mars apparently once had a rather extensive ocean and then lost it. This raises questions. How rapidly did Mars lose its ocean and why, and what may that loss portend for Earth?

We also do not completely understand the evolution of Earth's atmosphere, which was originally loaded with carbon dioxide (which would produce a bright red sky). About 800 million years ago, the oxygen content in the atmosphere was just about 1 percent of the total, enough to support the emergence of the first single-celled animals, the protozoa, but certainly not higher life forms.

This period in Earth's history led to an environmental event of great significance, namely a time when the entire Earth went into the deep freeze (the still-controversial *Snowball Earth* hypothesis). This may have resulted from a decrease in volcanism, a decline in the Sun's radiative output, or other events that would entail a sharp reduction in atmospheric CO_2 and a resulting drop in global temperature. Since ice ages are times of accelerated evolution, when the ice finally retreated, life on Earth was set for its Cambrian Explosion.

Fire and Ice

Today a major volcanic eruption is rare enough to make the news, but one billion years ago the Earth's crust still was immature and subject to huge bursts of volcanic activity. Such episodes poured incalculable volumes of gases and ash into the atmosphere, causing *mass depletions* leading to *mass extinctions* over a 500-million-year period. Earth's most recent experience with mass volcanism took place between 180 and 160 million years ago when the supercontinent Pangaea began to fracture. The *Pacific Ring of Fire* (text Figure 33-2) is but a trace of the paroxysm that marked the onset of Pangaea's breakup. Imagine what would have happened to humanity if there had been more than 6 billion of us on Pangaea.

Whether or not the Snowball Earth hypothesis turns into a tenable theory, there is no doubt that our planet plunges into frigid conditions called *ice ages* time and again. During the Permian Period, just 290 million years ago, when Pangaea was still a supercontinent, the Dvyka Ice Age cooled the entire planet, particularly the southern landmass of Pangaea (Gondwana). The Permian thus ended with the worst of the Earth's three great extinctions.

During the Mesozoic Era, which opened about 250 million years ago, tropical warmth re-placed Arctic cold on the post-ice-age planet. Moisture and precipitation abounded, atmospheric oxygen increased, and the Earth was ready for the faunal exuberance of the Jurassic. It seemed that only another ice age could halt the Mesozoic's profusion.

As it turns out, the last period of the Mesozoic, the Cretaceous, ended not with an ice age but as a result of a visit from a space traveler. About 65 million years ago the Earth was struck a glancing blow by a carbonaceous meteorite. While North America was worst hit, the impact affected the entire world. This event is identified in the geologic time record (Table 33-1) as the *KT boundary* (Cretaceous-Tertiary), and it marks the start of the sequence of events that led to the appearance of *Homo sapiens* on Earth.

Back to the Future

The 65 million years that have passed since the great extinction at the KT boundary have witnessed continued fluctuation, both major and minor, in the Earth's environment. Ice ages and volcanic eruptions have affected our planet with temporal and spatial differences, resulting in the disappearance of some species and the appearance, or change, of others.

About 110,000 years ago a warming phase occurred in the Pleistocene glaciation and, ac-cording to some scientists, *Homo sapiens* appeared on the scene, spreading first into Eurasia and later around the world. Taking advantage of milder times between Pleistocene cold periods, human communities expanded their frontiers while surviving the catastrophe of the Toba volcano about 73,500 years ago, considered the greatest threat to our existence ever to come from any source.

In the last 18,000 years, Earth and its human inhabitants have experienced atmospheric and volcanic events that, while not species-threatening on a global scale, clearly demonstrate that our planet is not much more environmentally stable today that it was in the past. Perhaps the greatest unknown presently facing humanity is the extent of the impact increasing numbers of humans will have on the environment that supports us. A second concern is that catastrophe has visited Earth in the past, and certainly will do so in the future, and the more than 6 billion humans on Earth today have no real experience with such events. Compared to other species, *Homo sapiens* has been the dominant species for only a short span of Earth's long history; and our future is precarious enough without our own actions shortening that future.

CHAPTER QUIZ

MULTIPLE-CHOICE QUESTIONS

1. Life appeared on Earth only recently in geologic time, and since then it has evolved through how many environmentally induced mass extinctions.
   a. six
   b. five
   c. four
   d. three

2. If the age of the Earth were compared to a person about 20 years of age, one hour of that person's life would equal approximately how many years of Earth history.
   a. 10,000
   b. 20,000
   c. 30,000
   d. 40,000

3. Originally, the Earth's atmosphere was loaded with the gas:
   a. carbon monoxide
   b. carbon dioxide
   c. oxygen
   d. nitrogen

4. The last (most recent) period of the Mesozoic era was the:
   a. Cretaceous
   b. Triassic
   c. Jurassic
   d. Permian

5. During the Pleistocene, the great drama of hominid evolution was proceeding in:
   a. Asia
   b. Europe
   c. Africa
   d. Australia

6. The most recent glaciation of the Pleistocene was the __?__ Glaciation.
   a. Wisconsinan
   b. Kansan
   c. Nebraskan
   d. Illinoian

7. The greatest threat to human existence to come from any source was a volcanic eruption occurring about 73,500 years ago. The volcano was called:
   a. Santorini
   b. Toba
   c. Tambora
   d. Krakatoa

8. This empire unified Europe as never before or since and put an indelible stamp on much of it.
   a. Mongol
   b. Hapsburg
   c. Han
   d. Roman

9. The Little Ice Age began to affect Europe in which century.
   a. thirteenth
   b. fourteenth
   c. fifteenth
   d. sixteenth

10. When the Little Ice Age came to its end in the mid-nineteenth-century, which of the following was **not** occurring.
    a. The Industrial Revolution was gathering steam.
    b. Colonization was transforming societies around the world.
    c. Population growth was slowing.
    d. Europeans were populating and dominating distant lands.

TRUE/FALSE QUESTIONS

1. Climatic fluctuations during the past 1000 years created environmental challenges that influenced the development of societies primarily in the Eastern Hemisphere. (TF)

2. The latest breakup of the supercontinent Pangaea began only 180 million years ago. (TF)

3. Ice ages are times of accelerated evolution. (TF)

4. The so-called "KT" boundary marks the start of the sequence of events that led to the appearance of *Homo sapiens* on this planet. (TF)

5. Throughout much of the Paleocene Epoch the planet was much colder than it had been during the time of the dinosaurs. (TF)

6. The hominid *Homo erectus* was the successor to *Australopithecus* and was in turn succeeded by *Homo sapiens*. (TF)

7. The warming period known as the Medieval Optimum began about 2000 years ago. (TF)

8. The Han Dynasty brought a golden age of expansion, consolidation, architecture, and art to China. (TF)

9. In North America, our growing understanding of the Little Ice Age helps explain why the Jamestown colony collapsed so fast. (TF)

10. The warming of the so-called Industrial Optimum was interrupted between 1910 and 1940. (TF)

STUDY QUESTIONS

1. Volcanic eruptions have had a dramatic impact on the history of our planet. Using a good outline map of the world, locate all the major volcanic eruptions cited in this chapter and identify them by name on the map in the same color. Next, using text Figure 4-1, shade in the major areas of world population in a different color. What do you think the impact of such volcanic activity would be today? Are there any obvious relationships with the Pacific Ring of Fire? How many countries would be affected? Estimate the number of humans displaced using census data for the different countries affected.

2. Ice ages are the other natural event that has affected the Earth's living space. Using a second world outline map and text Figures 4-1 and 33-5, shade in the areas covered by glacial ice in one color and the areas of major population concentration in another. What areas would be lost to human occupancy if such glaciation were repeated today? Using census data for individual countries, estimate the numbers of humans displaced. How are the areas and numbers different from the results you saw in question 1?

3. Using the results you obtained from questions 1 and 2, write a short report comparing the probable impacts of glaciation and volcanic eruptions on humanity today. Are there any areas that would remain habitable? Which continent would probably suffer the most?

Notes

Notes

Notes

CHAPTER 34.   PATTERNS AND PROCESSES OF ENVIRONMENTAL CHANGE

CHAPTER INTRODUCTION

As Earth's population continues to climb, there is more and more concern about the stress humanity places on the global environment. Resources, after all, are finite (nonrenewable) in many cases, and even those that are renewable have limits. Water, for example, is more likely than oil to be the cause of the next conflict in the Middle East. We face a new millennium with a world that is changed politically, economically, socially, and technologically from just a few decades ago. Much of this so-called advancement has been achieved with an extraordinary increase in the utilization of resources and environmental impact.

Consider how much the world has changed in just the past ten years during which the world map has been redrawn. New countries have arisen from old ones. New names by the hundreds have appeared on regional maps. New economic and political alliances have been formed. New industrial regions and new trade routes have emerged.

All this is going on against a background of global environmental change whose future is uncertain but troubling. A combination of natural cycles and human impacts may produce unprecedented climatic extremes. Climatic change, sometimes severe and dramatic, has been a natural part of Earth's cycles over time, but never before have these changes taken place with more than 6 billion human beings present who depend on a hospitable environment for survival.

Alteration of Ecosystems

Human alteration of the environment has been taking place for millennia, beginning with the use of fire to kill entire herds of animals, or the hunting to extinction of entire species of large mammals. Native populations from New Zealand to the Pacific Islands did significant damage to the flora and fauna long before the appearance of Europeans. Europeans, in turn, ravaged species ranging from Galapagos turtles to Arctic seals, North American Bison, and African species from snakes to leopards. Traditional as well as modern societies have had devastating impacts on their *ecosystems* (ecological units consisting of self-regulating associations of living and nonliving natural elements) as well as on those areas into which they migrate.

For the first time in history the combined impact of humanity's destructive and exploitive actions is capable of producing environmental changes at the global scale. Early human societies had relatively small populations, and their impacts on the physical environment were limited in both duration and intensity. Over the last 500 years, however, both the rate and scale at which humans modify the Earth have increased dramatically, particularly during the last half or the twentieth century.

Water

Water is a renewable resource, but water shortages threaten many parts of the world, including portions of the United States. The available supply of fresh water is not distributed evenly across the globe, as text Figure 1-5 shows. The largest totals are recorded in tropical areas of the world. The distribution is sustained through the *hydrologic cycle*, which brings moisture from the oceans to the landmasses (text Figure 34-1). Despite what you might think, the supply of water is anything but plentiful for the world as a whole. Chronic water shortages afflict farmers in Africa, and city dwellers in Southern California, Florida, and Spain. In many areas of the world people have congregated in places where water supplies are insufficient or undependable, and as human populations have expanded, people have increasingly settled in arid regions. Since nearly three-quarters of all the fresh water used annually is consumed in farming, the implications are considerable as a comparison of text Figures 1-5 and 4-1 reveals. Future conflicts over water supplies may come to rival recent conflicts over oil supplies. The next war in the Middle East, for example, could well be over water.

The Atmosphere

The Earth has only one *atmosphere*, a thin layer of air directly above the lands and oceans that we depend on for our survival. The atmosphere has a truly amazing capacity to cleanse itself, at least from some pollutants as it has done in the past after violent volcanic eruptions, but human pollution of the atmosphere may result in long-lasting, possibly even permanent damage. Some of the waste pouring into the atmosphere may be producing irreversible change to both the lower-level *troposphere* and the upper-level *stratosphere*. Human activity has produced an unprecedented concentration of greenhouse gases in the atmosphere, raising concerns about the prospects for significant global warming, and the full effect may not be felt until well into the present century.

The Land

Over the centuries human population growth has put increasing pressure on the land surface. The human impact on the Earth's land surface has several key aspects. One of the most significant is *desertification*, which is the encroachment of desert conditions on moister zones along the desert margins (text Figure 34-5). A second critical impact is *deforestation*, as the world's forests yield to human population pressure. Population pressure has also produced *soil erosion*, which has been called a "silent crisis" of global proportions. Finally, it is a sign of the times that the rapid accumulation of solid, toxic, and radioactive wastes in the technologically advanced countries is producing an increasingly serious disposal problem. As we enter the twenty-first century the Earth is under human assault as never before, and the well-being of humanity may well depend on how these and other critical issues are addressed.

CHAPTER QUIZ

MULTIPLE-CHOICE QUESTIONS

1. Biologists estimate that there may be as many as __?__ million types of organisms on Earth.
   a. 40
   b. 30
   c. 25
   d. 35

2. Human alteration of the physical world has become truly global during the past __?__ years.
   a. 25
   b. 50
   c. 75
   d. 100

3. Which of the following is **not** one of the world regions with the highest precipitation totals.
   a. South Asia
   b. Middle America
   c. Southeast Asia
   d. South Africa

4. In the Unites States, it is estimated that there is 50 times as much water stored in __?__ as falls as precipitation on the land surface.
   a. aquifers
   b. reservoirs
   c. lakes
   d. rivers

5. For the world as a whole, the greatest use of water is for:
   a. urban dwellers
   b. industry
   c. farming
   d. recreation

6. The lowest layer of the atmosphere is called the:
   a. ionosphere
   b. stratosphere
   c. tropopause
   d. troposphere

7. This body of water in the former Soviet Union has been virtually destroyed by irrigation diversion.
   a. the Aral Sea
   b. the Black Sea
   c. the Caspian Sea
   d. Lake Baikal

8. The United States enacted legislation establishing minimal clean-air standards in:
   a. 1950
   b. 1970
   c. 1960
   d. 1980

9. Which continent has the largest percentage of its area threatened by desertification.
   a. North America
   b. Africa
   c. Australia
   d. Asia

10. Which of the following is **not** a region where the largest areas of forest still survive.
   a. South America
   b. Southeast Asia
   c. Africa
   d. North America

TRUE/FALSE QUESTIONS

1. Humankind had **not** altered the environment until the start of the Industrial Revolution. (TF)

2. Water is a renewable resource. (TF)

3. The hydrologic cycle is the process that fills Earth's lakes and streams. (TF)

4. The atmosphere will probably still be able to clean itself even with all the human pollution pouring into it. (TF)

5. In the United States and Western Europe, reduced emissions into the air are not having any positive effect on reducing acid rain damage in forests or lakes. (TF)

6. Desertification can result from both human and natural causes. (TF)

7. Old trees in forests should be harvested first so the younger second-growth trees can provide habitat for birds and animals. (TF)

8. As the world's population grows, more marginal land is farmed. This practice leads to more soil erosion. (TF)

9. The United States produces more solid waste than any other country in the world. (TF)

10. The category of toxic waste includes radioactive waste. (TF)

STUDY QUESTIONS

1. When did humankind begin altering the environment? Human need for fresh water is putting great stress Earth's available supply. List the ways humans are creating this stress. What are the results? Look at text Figure 34-4 and read the text material about water problems in the Middle East. Using this information and other examples in the text, list places conflict might occur over water rights and usage.

2. How is pollution affecting our atmosphere? Can we reverse this process?

3. List the stresses put on the land by humans. What are the consequences listed? Do you think we can reverse this process? Be sure to cover desertification, deforestation, and soil erosion.

4. What problems has waste disposal created? Discuss toxic and radioactive waste disposal problems.

5. How has human impact affected the biodiversity on Earth? Is this a new phenomenon?

Notes

Notes

CHAPTER 35. CONFRONTING HUMAN-INDUCED GLOBAL ENVIRONMENTAL CHANGE

CHAPTER INTRODUCTION

Human alteration of the environment is nothing new. The ancient Greeks and Romans cut down many of the trees of the Mediterranean region and herds of goats decimated the lesser vegetation of the same area. Spanish invaders harvested the forests of Mexico for building materials and firewood. The difference is that in the modern era the combined impact of expanded human populations, increased consumption, and technological advances has led to environmental changes that some experts view as *irreversible*.

Environmental change has natural as well as human causes, and changes in the physical world are not always wrought by humans. Nature has its own cycles of change, and it is sometimes difficult to determine whether an observed change is attributed to nature or to humans. Current concerns over environmental change reflect humanity's role in accelerating the pace and extent of environmental change. For all the power of nature, humans are now the dominant species on the planet, and observed changes in Earth's physical systems are being influenced if not driven by human activities.

Understanding Environmental Change

Geography is one of the few academic disciplines in which the relationship between humans and the environment is a primary concern. In the past, textbooks and conferences involving geographers have focused primarily on local and regional changes, since these were perceived as the principal concerns. Today, things are different. A recent symposium led by geographers on "The Earth as Transformed by Human Action" addressed global environmental change as the now-recognized focus of concern. The geographer's concern with how things are organized on the Earth and how they are connected in space provides a useful platform from which to consider human-induced environmental change.

As the study of environmental change has moved forward, one important lesson that has been learned is that the global environmental systems are interconnected at numerous temporal and spatial scales. Human actions—the activities we undertake individually and collectively—are increasingly important factors in all sorts of global environmental changes. In the past, many of the environmental problems that drew our attention occurred at local or regional levels. Recent global environmental changes have forced us to recognize the larger spatial scales at which many processes operate.

Several interrelated factors are responsible for the accelerated impact of humans on the environment over the past two centuries. There can be little doubt, for example, that the fourfold increase in the *human population* in the twentieth century had significant environmental impact. Another is *consumption*, which has increased dramatically in parts of the modern world. Finally, *technology* has both expanded the human capacity to alter the environment and brought with it increasing energy demands.

Patterns of Consumption

While the population of countries in the developed core are often smaller than those in the periphery, per capita consumption of resources in the rich countries is far greater. Maps of world population fail to convey the relative demands made by different peoples on the Earth's resources.

Consequently, it is important to keep in mind that many societies consume resources at a level and rate that far exceed basic subsistence needs, a level many times that of people in poorer countries. Thus rapid population growth in the poorer countries tends to be a local or regional matter, keeping rural areas mired in poverty. But population growth in the richer countries is also a matter of concern, one whose impact is not just local or regional but global. This underscores the importance of thinking geographically about humans and the environment.

Transportation

Global consumption is tied to technology, and modes of transportation represent some of the most important technological advances in human history. The Industrial Revolution, you are reminded, was essentially a revolution in transportation that required increased resource use. Resources are needed not only to make the actual vehicles that move people and goods, but also to build and maintain the related infrastructure—roads, railroad tracks, repair facilities, and the like. And with each innovation the impacts seem to widen. Moreover, transportation innovations offer access to remote areas of the planet and these places, in turn, have been altered by human activity. Modern transportation devices thus contribute to environmental change not just by consuming energy, producing pollution, and indirectly contributing to alteration of even remote areas, but by facilitating global trade networks that fuel consumption in the developed core.

Policy Responses to Environmental Change

A major challenge in confronting environmental problems is that many of these problems do not lie within a single jurisdiction. Environmental problems frequently cross political boundaries, complicating regulation and management efforts. Designing policy responses is thus complicated by the fact that the political map does not reflect the geography of environmental issues. There are few international policy-making bodies with significant authority over multinational environmental spaces. Those that do exist often have limited authority and must heed the concerns of member states. Nonetheless, increasing recognition of the gravity of certain problems has resulted in a number of international accords being adopted on issues ranging from biodiversity to climatic change.

CHAPTER QUIZ

MULTIPLE-CHOICE QUESTIONS

1. Approximately __?__ percent of all the species that have ever existed on our planet have evolved and become extinct.
    a. 65
    b. 85
    c. 95
    d. 75

2. Because of humans, the current rate of the extinction of species is estimated to be __?__ times faster than natural extinction rates.
    a. 2,000 to 8,000
    b. 1,000 to 10,000
    c. 3,000 to 9,000
    d. 4,000 to 12,000

3. In the twentieth century the human population increased:
   a. twofold
   b. eightfold
   c. tenfold
   d. fourfold

4. It is estimated that a baby born in the U.S. today will consume __?__ times as much energy over a lifetime as a baby born in Bangladesh.
   a. 250
   b. 350
   c. 450
   d. 750

5. Globally, the consumption of resources is tied to:
   a. population numbers
   b. technology
   c. local availability
   d. cost

6. The naturally occurring *ozone layer* found in the atmosphere is of vital importance because it protects the Earth from the sun's harmful ultraviolet rays. The layer of the atmosphere where this ozone layer is found is the:
   a. tropopause
   b. thermosphere
   c. troposphere
   d. stratosphere

7. In 1999, the production of global energy was __?__ percent greater than in 1971.
   a. 25
   b. 50
   c. 75
   d. 100

8. Chlorofluorocarbon gases (CFCs), which have been found to damage the Earth's ozone layer, have only been in use since the:
   a. 1950s
   b. 1960s
   c. 1970s
   d. 1980s

9. Modern societies may draw resources from all over the world, yet it is estimated a hunter-gatherer could subsist on the resources found within an area of about __?__ square kilometers.
   a. 13
   b. 26
   c. 54
   d. 67

10. Consumption of material goods is closely linked to consumption of:
    a. raw materials
    b. water
    c. energy
    d. food stuffs

TRUE/FALSE QUESTIONS

1. Regional environmental changes can have global effects. (TF)

2. Because wealthier countries consume more of the world's resources, population growth in these countries has a greater impact on the environment than it does in poorer countries. (TF)

3. The demand for hamburger meat in the United States has a direct impact on the cutting of forests in Central and South America. (TF)

4. Technology has played a large role in destroying the environment around the world. (TF)

5. Transportation has allowed access to remote places, causing erosion because of dirt roads. (TF)

6. Ships unintentionally transport different species of sea life from one part of the world to another. (TF)

7. Fossil fuels are a renewable resource. (TF)

8. GIS is a valuable tool in helping to analyze data on global change in new and useful ways. (TF)

9. The ozone layer over Antarctica has thinned and now has a hole in it that is growing. (TF)

10. While some global changes are "chaotic" and many are nonlinear, modern computers are able to unravel the mysteries and do a good job of reliably predicting future conditions. (TF)

STUDY QUESTIONS

1. There are many things to consider when we try to understand humanity's role in environmental change. List the factors involved and give examples of each. Include the damage done.

2. Look at text Figures 35-1 and 35-2. Can you understand why oil slicks appear in this pattern? What causes these oil slicks? What are some alternative sources for energy besides the use of fossil fuels?

3. Pollution is a worldwide problem. What organizations are trying to address this problem? What progress is being made? What issues are being addressed? What are some of the results that could be seen from global climate change? Why must these problems be addressed now?

Notes

Notes

226

STUDY GUIDE ANSWER SECTION

CH#	MULTIPLE-CHOICE	TRUE/FALSE
1.	1c, 2c, 3b, 4c, 5a, 6c, 7d, 8c, 9a, 10b	1T, 2F, 3F, 4T, 5F, 6F, 7T, 8F, 9F, 10F
2.	1b, 2c, 3a, 4c, 5c, 6b, 7b, 8c, 9b, 10c	1F, 2T, 3F, 4T, 5F, 6T, 7F, 8T, 9T, 10F
3.	1a, 2b, 3c, 4b, 5c, 6a, 7c, 8c, 9a, 10b	1F, 2F, 3T, 4F, 5T, 6F, 7T, 8F, 9F, 10T
4.	1b, 2b, 3c, 4d, 5b, 6a, 7d, 8c, 9d, 10c	1F, 2F, 3F, 4T, 5T, 6T, 7F, 8T, 9F, 10T
5.	1d, 2b, 3c, 4d, 5d, 6a, 7d, 8b, 9a, 10b	1F, 2T, 3T, 4F, 5T, 6T, 7F, 8T, 9T, 10F
6.	1b, 2a, 3d, 4c, 5d, 6a, 7c, 8b, 9a, 10d	1F, 2F, 3T, 4F, 5T, 6T, 7F, 8T, 9F, 10F
7.	1b, 2c, 3a, 4d, 5b, 6a, 7c, 8b, 9d, 10a	1F, 2F, 3F, 4T, 5T, 6F, 7T, 8F, 9T, 10F
8.	1c, 2a, 3b, 4c, 5c, 6b, 7a, 8d, 9a, 10b	1F, 2F, 3F, 4F, 5T, 6T, 7T, 8T, 9T, 10F
9.	1c, 2c, 3d, 4a, 5b, 6c, 7d, 8b, 9a, 10c	1T, 2F, 3F, 4F, 5T, 6F, 7T, 8F, 9T, 10T
10.	1a, 2b, 3a, 4b, 5c, 6d, 7d, 8a, 9c, 10c	1T, 2F, 3T, 4T, 5T, 6F, 7F, 8T, 9T, 10T
11.	1b, 2c, 3d, 4a, 5a, 6b, 7c, 8d, 9c, 10b	1F, 2F, 3T, 4T, 5T, 6F, 7F, 8T, 9F, 10T
12.	1d, 2a, 3c, 4b, 5d, 6b, 7a, 8c, 9d, 10a	1F, 2T, 3F, 4T, 5F, 6T, 7T, 8T, 9T, 10T
13.	1c, 2d, 3b, 4a, 5a, 6b, 7d, 8c, 9c, 10b	1F, 2F, 3F, 4F, 5F, 6T, 7T, 8F, 9T, 10T
14.	1c, 2a, 3d, 4b, 5c, 6d, 7d, 8b, 9c, 10a	1F, 2T, 3T, 4T, 5T, 6F, 7F, 8F, 9T, 10F
15.	1d, 2b, 3c, 4b, 5d, 6c, 7b, 8b, 9d, 10a	1F, 2F, 3T, 4F, 5T, 6F, 7T, 8F, 9T, 10T
16.	1a, 2c, 3b, 4d, 5a, 6c, 7b, 8d, 9a, 10c	1T, 2F, 3T, 4F, 5T, 6T, 7T, 8F, 9F, 10T
17.	1b, 2d, 3a, 4c, 5b, 6d, 7b, 8d, 9c, 10a	1T, 2T, 3F, 4T, 5T, 6F, 7F, 8T, 9T, 10F
18.	1c, 2c, 3b, 4d, 5b, 6c, 7a, 8d, 9b, 10b	1F, 2F, 3T, 4T, 5F, 6T, 7F, 8T, 9F, 10T
19.	1a, 2c, 3b, 4d, 5a, 6c, 7b, 8c, 9c, 10b	1F, 2F, 3T, 4T, 5T, 6T, 7F, 8T, 9T, 10T
20.	1b, 2c, 3c, 4c, 5d, 6a, 7c, 8b, 9c, 10b,	1F, 2F, 3F, 4T, 5T, 6T, 7T, 8F, 9T, 10F
21.	1a, 2b, 3d, 4b, 5c, 6a, 7d, 8b, 9c, 10c	1T, 2T, 3F, 4T, 5F, 6T, 7T, 8T, 9T, 10F
22.	1b, 2b, 3d, 4a, 5c, 6d, 7d, 8a, 9d, 10a	1T, 2T, 3T, 4F, 5T, 6F, 7F, 8T, 9F, 10F
23.	1a, 2b, 3b, 4c, 5c, 6b, 7a, 8d, 9c, 10b	1T, 2F, 3T, 4T, 5F, 6T, 7F, 8T, 9T, 10T
24.	1a, 2d, 3c, 4b, 5d, 6a, 7c, 8b, 9d, 10a	1F, 2F, 3F, 4T, 5T, 6F, 7T, 8T, 9F, 10F
25.	1b, 2c, 3d, 4a, 5b, 6a, 7d, 8c, 9b, 10d	1F, 2T, 3T, 4F, 5F, 6T, 7F, 8T, 9F, 10T
26.	1c, 2b, 3d, 4c, 5a, 6b, 7c, 8b, 9c, 10a	1T, 2F, 3T, 4F, 5F, 6T, 7F, 8F, 9T, 10T
27.	1b, 2d, 3c, 4a, 5b, 6c, 7d, 8b, 9a, 10c	1F, 2F, 3T, 4T, 5F, 6T, 7T, 8F, 9T, 19T
28.	1b, 2c, 3d, 4a, 5c, 6b, 7d, 8a, 9c, 10b	1F, 2T, 3T, 5F, 5T, 6T, 7T, 8T, 9F, 10F

29. 1b, 2c, 3d, 4a, 5b, 6d 7c, 8a, 9b, 10d	1T, 2F, 3T, 4T, 5F, 6T, 7T, 8F, 9T, 10F
30. 1b, 2d, 3c, 4a, 5b, 6c, 7a, 8b, 9a, 10c	1T, 2F, 3F, 4T, 5T, 6F, 7T, 8F, 9F, 10T
31. 1b, 2d, 3c, 4a, 6d, 6b, 7c, 8a, 9d, 10b	1T, 2T, 3F, 4T, 5F, 6T, 7F, 8T, 9F, 10F
32. 1b, 2d, 3c, 4b, 5a, 6d, 7b, 8c, 9c, 10a	1F, 2T, 3F, 4T, 5F, 6T, 7F, 8F, 9T, 10T
33. 1d, 2c, 3b, 4a, 5c, 6a, 7b, 8d, 9b, 10c	1F, 2T, 3T, 4T, 5F, 6T, 7T, 8F, 9T, 10F
34. 1a, 2b, 3d, 4a, 5c, 6d, 7a, 8b, 9c, 10d	1F, 2T, 3T, 4F, 5F, 6T, 7F, 8T, 9T, 10F
35. 1c, 2b, 3d, 4a, 5b, 6d, 7c, 8a, 9b, 10c	1T, 2T, 3T, 4T, 5F, 6T, 7F, 8T, 9T, 10F

Notes

Notes

Notes

Notes